four
powerful
principles
for
change

Jesus
LORD OF YOUR
personAlity

BOB RUSSELL
with Rusty Russell

HOWARD
PUBLISHING CO.

Our purpose at Howard Publishing is to:

- *Increase faith* in the hearts of growing Christians
- *Inspire holiness* in the lives of believers
- *Instill hope* in the hearts of struggling people everywhere

Because He's coming again!

Jesus, Lord of Your Personality
© 2002 by Bob Russell with Rusty Russell
All rights reserved. Printed in the United States of America
Published by Howard Publishing Co., Inc.
3117 North 7th Street, West Monroe, Louisiana 71291-2227

02 03 04 05 06 07 08 09 10 11   10 9 8 7 6 5 4 3 2 1

Edited by Dawn M. Brandon
Interior design by John Luke
Cover design by LinDee Loveland

Library of Congress Cataloging-in-Publication Data
Russell, Bob, 1943-
    Jesus, Lord of your personality : four powerful principles for change / Bob
Russell with Rusty Russell.
       p. cm.
    Includes bibliographical references.
    ISBN: 1-58229-252-3
    1. Christian life. 2. Gratitude. I. Russell, Rusty, 1967- II. Title.
BV4501.3 .R87 2002
248.4—dc21   2002024273

Italics in scriptures were added by the author for emphasis. Scripture quotations not otherwise marked are taken from the HOLY BIBLE, NEW INTERNATIONAL VERSION®. Copyright © 1973, 1978, 1984 by International Bible Society. Used by permission of Zondervan Publishing House. Other scriptures are quoted from *The Holy Bible*, Authorized King James Version (KJV), © 1961 by The National Publishing Co.; *The Living Bible* (TLB), © 1971 by Tyndale House Publishers, Inc.; *The Message* (MSG), © 1994 by Eugene H. Peterson, NavPress. All rights reserved.

DEDICATION

To my wife, Judy, who has always
been a joy to live with!

contents

ACKNOWLEDGMENTS

Rusty and I have been blessed with a great support staff, Debbie Carper and Barbara Dabney, which is why we are able to preach and write and keep our sanity. Several preachers contributed illustrations for this book, including Dave Stone and Dave Kennedy on our staff and Mark Jones at First Christian Church in Columbus, Indiana. Our interns Brian Heckber and Herbie Miller worked hard to track down the details of quotes and stories in an effort to do all things with excellence.

We feel honored to be producing our second book with Howard Publishing. It is a joy to work with Denny and Philis Boultinghouse. We look forward to doing another book with Howard, especially if they'll hire Dawn Brandon again to be our editor! She did a superb job.

Whenever we agree to write a book, our family members know they will be asked to make certain concessions and sacrifices. We both are grateful for our very supportive wives, Judy and Kellie, and for the rest of our family members whom we love so much—Phil, Lisa, Corrie, Charlie, Tommy, and Kimberly. We hope we can model the heart and personality of Christ for each of you. Thanks for loving us even though you know our personalities are still in need of some transformation!

INTRODUCTION

Years ago I walked into the house as the phone was ringing. I rushed to answer it, but just as I picked up the receiver the answering machine came on. I shouted, "Hello!" over the greeting and heard my wife's voice on the other end of the line. "Hold on!" I said, and we both waited until the recorded message ended before we started our conversation.

You need to understand my wife, Judy. She has a very steady personality. She's kind of like Jesus; she's "the same yesterday, today and forever"! There aren't many ups and downs to her attitude. She doesn't get enthusiastic about many things, but she seldom goes into depression either.

She is consistently joyful, upbeat, and pleasant to be around. She's extremely easy to live with. And her voice on the phone always has a cheery tone to it.

My personality tends to fluctuate much more often. I can be jubilant one moment and dejected the next. I can be gentle, upbeat, and positive with strangers, but at home I can be boring, anxious, and even morose.

After a brief discussion, we hung up the phone. I didn't realize the recorder had taped the conversation in its entirety. Several hours later, I noticed there was a message on the answering machine and pushed the replay button. I couldn't get over the contrast between my wife's tone and mine. I sounded so glum! So boring!

Judy said a cheery "Hello!" and asked, "Is everything OK?"

"Yeah," I mumbled.

"We got delayed at work, and I just wanted you to know I'm going to be a little late," she said with a lilt.

"OK," I grunted.

"Did you have a good day?" she asked, obviously trying to see if there was a quiver of life in me.

"Fine," I mumbled.

"Well, I'll be there in a few minutes!"

"All right," I grunted.

When I heard the tone of my voice and my lack of enthusiasm, I couldn't believe it. I felt terrible! Do I really sound like that? Am I that unenthusiastic all the time? Is my personality that morose and gloomy? What's it like to have to live with *me* every day?

I then recalled a chapter in Bruce Larson's book *Dare to Live Now* titled "Are You Fun to Live With?" I realized at that moment that I wasn't much fun to be around at times. Even though I'm a Christian and I love the Lord, and even though I love my family, that love seldom is reflected in the way I respond to the people closest to me.

I determined that day to improve my "at home" personality. I asked Jesus Christ to become the Lord of my personality. There was no gross sin in my life that needed to be eliminated, but my personality needed an overhaul. Over the years the Lord has slowly helped change my personality at home. I laugh more and am less uptight. I am more focused and less preoccupied. I don't pout as much, and I'm quicker to tease and have fun.

As a result, my public persona is much more relaxed and genuine. I still have a long way to go, but I'm improving. There's an old song that says, "I'm not what I ought to be, I'm not what I'm going to be, but thank God I'm not what I used to be!"

When my son Rusty was in elementary school, he was given a creative writing assignment—he had to complete the sentence "I love it when..." He wrote, "I love it when my dad laughs." I was delighted! I want our home to be a place of laughter and joy, not a place of complaining, worrying, moodiness, and bitterness. And I know that whether we successfully create that positive mood in our home depends a lot on my attitude.

What is it like to live with you? Is your personality full of joy, peace, and contentment? Or are you a bear to live with? Do people tiptoe on eggshells around you, hoping not to upset you?

The Bible promises, "Therefore, if anyone is in Christ, he is a new creation; the old has gone, the new has come!" (2 Corinthians 5:17). Jesus Christ wants to make you a new creature from the inside out. He wants to do more than prevent you from getting drunk, having an affair, or robbing a bank. Jesus wants to be Lord of your personality. He wants to change your attitude. He wants to develop a mature personality in you. He wants to make you pleasant to live with. He wants your personality to be contagious to unbelievers. When you begin to radiate the abundant life in Christ, you are able to make Christ more attractive to your children and to those you meet in the marketplace.

Southwest Airlines has a slogan: "We Hire Attitudes." They describe an attitude as "listening, caring, smiling, and saying 'thank you.'" Wouldn't you like to be that kind of person—the kind of person people want to be around, whom people want to hire in successful organizations? You might say, "I don't have the energy. I don't have it in me to be that kind of person. I'm not wired like that." Well, you're probably right. But Jesus Christ can transform your personality.

introduction

David wrote in Psalm 30, "You turned my wailing into dancing; you removed my sackcloth and clothed me with joy, that my heart may sing to you and not be silent. O LORD my God, I will give you thanks forever" (vv. 11–12). Jesus Christ wants to turn your wailing into dancing. But he won't do it the way you might think. He isn't going to give you more of this world's things. In fact, that could be counterproductive. A lot of people obtain just about all this world could offer and become more miserable. Instead, Christ wants to change your attitude.

A member of our church wrote to me about a friend of hers who had a problem. "My friend Ann asked me to pray with her that God would intervene and change the conditions at work," she wrote. Ann's new boss, Janet, was harsh and often humiliated those under her authority. Janet made the atmosphere stressful and full of strife. Her employees called her "Barracuda" behind her back.

The letter continued,

> We prayed Barracuda would be transferred to another department, or that my friend would be. One morning while I was in prayer, I was motivated to pray for the Barracuda's salvation. It was difficult to pray for her soul.... [I reasoned that] someone so hateful could never soften up enough to be touched by the Spirit of God.
>
> Not long after I prayed earnestly for her, I asked Ann how the Barracuda was doing. My friend said,

"Well, she's been very civil the past few days. She seems to have mellowed considerably." I kept praying and thanking God for the way he was working.

A few days later my friend called. "Guess what! The Barracuda came by my desk this morning, sat down with me and smiled and told me she had been baptized at her church Sunday morning! She is a new creature in Christ and a whole new personality!"[1]

Jesus said to his disciples, "I have told you this so that my joy may be in you and that your joy may be complete" (John 15:11). Jesus wants your joy to be complete. He doesn't want you to be gloomy, depressed, and bitter. When you have a sour attitude, it affects everyone around you in a negative way. That's not what Christ wants for you. He said, "I have come that they may have life, and have it to the full" (John 10:10). Can you imagine the impact you could have on those around you—especially those closest to you—if Jesus were Lord of your personality?

Max Lucado writes,

[God] wants us to be just like Jesus.

Isn't that good news? You aren't stuck with today's personality. You aren't condemned to "grumpydom." You are tweakable. Even if you've worried each day of your life, you needn't worry the rest of your life. So what if you were born a bigot? You don't have to die one.

Where did we get the idea we can't change? From

whence come statements such as "It's just my nature to worry" or "I'll always be pessimistic. I'm just that way...." Who says? Would we make similar statements about our bodies? "It's just my nature to have a broken leg. I can't do anything about it." Of course not. If our bodies malfunction, we seek help. Shouldn't we do the same with our hearts? Shouldn't we seek aid for our sour attitudes? Can't we request treatment for our selfish tirades? Of course we can. Jesus can change our hearts. He wants us to have a heart like his.[2]

I'm sure there are many things you could do to try to change your habits. In this book, we'll tackle what I believe are four of the most common inhibitors to a positive personality. If you allow Christ to give you an attitude adjustment in these four areas, you'll begin to look into the mirror and see a new person. Yielding to Jesus as Lord of your personality will make you the kind of person others enjoy being with.

Let us please God by

serving him with

thankful hearts.

—*Hebrews* 12:28 *TLB*

Were not ten healed?
Where are the other nine?

—*Jesus Christ*

chapter 1

FROM griping TO grateful

A few years ago I invited my two grown sons and their new wives to accompany my wife, Judy, and me on a vacation. After I explained that I would pay for everything, they agreed to go. We borrowed a nice van, and the six of us spent a week driving to and from Niagara Falls, stopping at a few historical places and relatives' homes along the way. It was an expensive week, but we had a great time and created a lot of memories. I'll never forget what my daughters-in-law said to me as we drove back into our driveway. "Thanks for spoiling us this week," they said. They didn't have to say anything else. I fought back the tears. I felt like the trip was worth every dime because they had a good time, and because they were grateful. They could have complained if they had wanted to—about the long trip, the hot weather, putting up with relatives for a whole week, mediocre hotels…but instead they were grateful and acted like they had been spoiled for the week.

Would you rather spend a week with a constant complainer or someone who is thankful? Grumblers drain you of your energy, but a word of thanksgiving lifts you up. You never hear someone say, "Let's go visit him—I just love to hear him complain!"

WHERE ARE THE OTHER NINE?

Remember the ten lepers who came to Jesus to be healed? You think *your* life is tough! One scholar suggested that leprosy was the first-century equivalent of AIDS. Although leprosy was not related to sexual behavior, people today fear AIDS and shun people who have contracted the disease much like those in the first century avoided lepers. Leprosy was a terminal disease that slowly ate away at the nerve endings. Lepers often lost their extremities—their fingers, toes, and ears would be eaten away. They were disfigured and repulsive. Because their disease was contagious, lepers were forced to spend their lives quarantined from everyone—unable to live with family and loved ones, sentenced to exist in leper colonies, and required to call out, "Unclean! Unclean!" whenever an unsuspecting stranger drew near. You can understand why the lepers desperately wanted to be healed by Jesus.

> As he [Jesus] was going into a village, ten men who had leprosy met him. They stood at a distance and called out in a loud voice, "Jesus, Master, have pity on us!" When he saw them, he said, "Go, show yourselves to the priests." And as they went, they were cleansed. (Luke 17:12–14)

A young woman in our congregation recently had cancer surgery, followed by weeks of chemotherapy. It was a difficult time, but the other day her exuberant mother came up to me and said, "The latest tests revealed no cancer cells! They've declared my daughter cured! They don't want to see her for six months!" The entire family was jubilant, and it was fun to rejoice with them.

Imagine the joy those ten lepers suddenly experienced the moment they were healed. Their sores were gone! Their skin was clear! Their bodies were whole! Their features were normal! They must have celebrated with tears, embraces, shouts, and squeals of delight!

> One of them, when he saw he was healed, came back, praising God in a loud voice. He threw himself at Jesus' feet and thanked him—and he was a Samaritan. (Luke 17:15–16)

Only the Samaritan—the one from a despised race—

returned to Jesus to express thanks. Jesus was disappointed that only one returned, but he was pleased with the man's expression of thanks.

> Jesus asked, "Were not all ten cleansed? Where are the other nine? Was no one found to return and give praise to God except this foreigner?" Then he said to him, "Rise and go; your faith has made you well." (Luke 17:17–19)

Have you ever wondered why the other nine didn't return to thank Jesus? If you had been there and you could interview them, what would their excuses be? I had an imaginary conversation with all nine lepers who didn't return to Jesus, and here's what they told me:

Leper Number One said, "I went to show myself to the priest—I was just doing what I was told. I didn't think I should disobey orders." (Legalists aren't usually grateful people.)

Leper Number Two told me, "I immediately went to see my family. I've missed them so much! And they've been through a lot. By the time I finished celebrating with my family and friends, Jesus had left. I never got the chance to thank him."

"Of course I'm grateful," said Leper Number Three, "but I didn't know he expected praise. After all, he does that for a living! You don't send a thank-you note to your doctor, do you? He gets paid for it, right?"

Leper Number Four said, "To be real honest, I'm not sure it's to my advantage to be healed. Before, all I had to do was beg for a living. Now I have to get a real job. People used to feel sorry for me. Now they ignore me. I'm not sure it's that good of a deal to be healthy."

"I'm healed, but I'm not all that pleased with the way I look," replied Leper Number Five. "I had leprosy for fifteen years, and I look so much older than I did when I got the disease. I thought if he healed me, he would make me look a lot younger. He could have done more, you know."

Leper Number Six told me, "Sure, I'm cured. But I just can't rejoice when I know there are hundreds of lepers out there still isolated and lonely. I'd feel guilty celebrating when there's so much human suffering in the world."

Leper Number Seven promised, "Oh, I will thank him. I just haven't gotten around to it yet. I've been so busy since I was healed—talk shows, newspaper interviews... Later today all ten of us are having our picture taken for a 'Got Milk' billboard! Time's just been flying by!"

Leper Number Eight said, "I didn't go back and thank him because I'm afraid to. I'm grateful, but I've heard that Jesus can be really demanding. He asked one guy to sell everything he had, and he told another to take up his *cross* and follow him! I don't want to be that fanatical. I'm afraid he'll expect too much in return."

"I know I got better after talking to Jesus," replied Leper Number Nine, "but I think it might have been a coincidence. For several weeks prior to seeing Jesus I was taking some special herbs that were recommended for leprosy, and I'm not sure Jesus deserves all the credit."

WHERE ARE YOU?

What are your excuses? Why don't you regularly come to God with a grateful heart? See if any of these excuses fit you.

A Privileged Upbringing

Were you spoiled rotten as a child? If your parents and grandparents gave you almost everything you wanted, if you were pampered and protected, you probably have unrealistic expectations about life. You think life is supposed to be free of pain and disappointment. Therefore, whenever life is less than perfect, you focus on the negatives and miss the positives. When you move into a beautiful new house, you focus on that one imperfection in the carpet, and you gripe about the carpet installers. When you eat out at a wonderful restaurant, you complain that the waiter brought the main dish before you were finished with the salad. You had perfect seats for the orchestra but were so offended by the way the violinist blew his nose between movements that the whole night was ruined for you.

Affluent Experiences

Have you had a taste of the best this world has to offer? You went to Hawaii once on vacation, so now it's harder for you to enjoy the state park. You've eaten a steak at Ruth's Chris, so it's harder to be thankful for a meal at Ponderosa. You've driven a Jaguar, so now you can't be as content with your used Chevrolet. You've cheered for a national champion, so now it's difficult to be grateful when your team has a good season but doesn't take home the title.

Last Easter we had one of the best worship services I've ever been involved in. It was so inspirational that everyone in the building seemed moved. Throughout the weekend, people commented about how awesome the service was. One woman came up to me and said, "I've been to church all my life..." I was sure she was about to tell me that the service was the best worship experience she'd ever had. Instead, she scolded, "and that's the first Easter that we didn't sing 'Up from the Grave He Arose'!" She walked away in a huff. I was dumbfounded! She had become so used to outstanding worship services that she expected perfection (as she defined it) all the time!

Generally speaking, the more we have, the less grateful we are. It should be the opposite; the more we have, the more thankful we should be. But it usually doesn't work that way, does it?

A wise man prayed, "Give me neither poverty nor riches, but give me only my daily bread. Otherwise, I may have too much and disown you and say, 'Who is the LORD?' Or I may become poor and steal, and so dishonor the name of my God" (Proverbs 30:8–9).

It is a rare person who, when his cup frequently runs over, can give thanks to God instead of complaining about the limited size of his mug!

Negative Companions

Are all of your friends "grumpy old men"? Proverbs 13:20 says, "He who walks with the wise grows wise, but a companion of fools suffers harm." If your closest associates are grateful people, you're likely to become more thankful for what you have. If your closest friends are negative, critical complainers, you will soon emulate them.

Our church often takes large groups on short-term mission trips. Besides the primary goal of spreading the gospel of Christ, one of the greatest benefits of short-term mission trips is the fellowship and camaraderie that develops among the team members. However, our missions staff has learned that the wrong mix of people can have detrimental effects. So they do their best to avoid having two complainers on the same trip. The complainers tend to gravitate toward each other and feed off of one another. They exaggerate every minor inconvenience, contaminate others, and sour the trip for everyone. The Scripture warns, "Do not be misled: 'Bad company corrupts good character'" (1 Corinthians 15:33).

No matter how fulfilling your job, how spacious your house, how personable your mate, or how edifying your church might be; if you associate with people who are always finding fault, you soon will become a grumpy person. That's human nature.

Frequent Comparisons

Are you constantly comparing your circumstances with someone else's?

"Their kids are better behaved than ours."

"Her husband is more romantic than mine."

"Their house has a nicer backyard."

"Their church has a better preacher."

"His salary is much higher than mine."

<u>If you compare your circumstances with others who have it better, you'll become a thankless, unhappy person, because no matter how much you have, there will always be someone who has more.</u>

My wife, Judy, oversees The Living Word—our tape and radio ministry. Recently Max Lucado was our guest speaker. A few days after he spoke, Judy gleefully told me that they sold a record 670 tapes of Max's sermon.

I made the mistake of asking, "What's the highest number of tapes you've ever sold of one of my sermons?"

"Your message on 'worry' a few weeks ago sold 250 tapes," she answered.

If my wife had come to me the month before and said, "Your sermon on 'worry' touched so many people! We sold 250 tapes!" I would have been elated. But compared with 670 tapes, I felt as though mine hadn't sold diddly-squat!

One couple confessed that they often had compared their son with his best friend. His friend was studious, focused, and apparently headed for success. Their son was frivolous, disinterested in academics, and unmotivated. They would say, "Why can't Mark be more like his friend Jason?"

Then one day Jason's parents said to them, "We've really enjoyed having Mark around. He's good for Jason. We've often wished Jason were more like Mark. He's so personable, easygoing, and fun-loving. Our son is too serious."

The Bible says, "When they measure themselves by themselves and compare themselves with themselves, they are not wise" (2 Corinthians 10:12).

GRATITUDE IS THE KEY TO PERSONAL HAPPINESS

G. K. Chesterton called gratitude "the mother of all virtues." More than any other virtue, gratitude determines the degree of your happiness and contentment in life.

On a scale of one to ten, how happy are you right now? You might say, "Well, I'm about a 'two' on the happiness meter because of some of my circumstances." Or maybe you're at a seven or an eight—but you wouldn't say nine or ten because, after all, life's not perfect. You're convinced that if a few things were different in your life—maybe if you had more money, a nicer house, or a better relationship with your spouse—you'd be happier, right?

I'll bet I could make you exuberantly happy with your present circumstances within twenty-four hours. But it would be a *brutal* twenty-four hours! With a little help from your friends, here's what I'd put you through:

First, your lawyer would call to inform you that you are being sued; all your material possessions will be confiscated to cover the damages.

Then I would convince one of your closest friends to call and inform you that the five people you love the most had died tragically.

Then your doctor would call and tell you that your latest x-rays revealed a terminal disease.

Then I'd get one of your church members to inform you that the preacher has been pilfering money from the offerings, and the church is getting ready to fold.

Then the theologian you respect most would claim that the Bible is a hoax, God does not exist, and there is no hope of life after death.

At the end of the twenty-four hours, I would inform you that all those things you had just been told were not true. Your loved ones are alive, your possessions are intact, you still have your health, your church is not folding, and your hope in Christ is secure. After you punched me in the nose, you'd begin to celebrate all the good things God has given you!

Your circumstances didn't change, but your attitude did.

HOW TO CREATE A
NEW ATTITUDE OF GRATITUDE

You can become a grateful person without going through that kind of trauma. Jesus Christ is ready to begin changing your personality today, but you have to open yourself up to his transforming power. Let me suggest several spiritual exercises that will enable Christ to transform you from a grumbler to a person of gratitude.

(1.) ### Acknowledge That Everything You Have Is God's, Not Yours

Nothing you have is yours. It all belongs to the Lord. The Bible says, "The earth is the LORD's, and everything in it, the world, and all who live in it" (Psalm 24:1). God just loans you the things you have so you can be a steward for a little while. When you begin to grasp that concept, you'll gain a new appreciation for the things you've been given.

Let's suppose a wealthy man came to you with a request. He said to you:

> I'm going overseas on business, and I need someone to watch my estate. I'd like you to be my housesitter. I've arranged for someone to clean the house and

take care of the yard, but I want someone I can trust to live there so the house doesn't sit idle while I'm gone. You can live in my mansion, drive any of my cars—my BMW convertible, my SUV, or even one of the antiques. You can use my swimming pool anytime you want, and the entertainment center in the lower level of the house is for you to enjoy. I'll show you where the four-wheeler is, and you can take the boat out on the lake. I'm not sure how long I'll be gone. This kind of trip usually takes about six months, but it's hard to tell for sure. It might only be a couple of weeks, or I might be gone for two years. Until I get back, please enjoy yourself. What's mine is yours.

You agree to be the housesitter, and for four months you have the time of your life. You drive the BMW and the antiques, you enjoy the four-wheeler and the boat, and you frequently entertain your friends and family. After four months you receive notice that the owner is returning a little earlier than expected. How would you feel? Sure, you'd be disappointed that the fun was over. But would you feel cheated? Would you shake your fist at the owner and say, "How could you be so cruel and treat me so unfairly? You said six months! I deserve six months!"

I hope that's not how you would respond. More likely, you would say, "Thanks for a great four months. We had so much fun, and I'm so grateful!"

You don't own anything. God gives you the privilege of living in this world for a little while and enjoying its benefits. He doesn't tell you exactly when the privilege will end, and he doesn't promise you any day beyond today. But God goes one step further than the owner of that house did. He offers to adopt you as his child. He wants you to enjoy his estate while you're here on this earth; then when he returns, he wants you to move in with him! He's preparing for you an even finer existence in the future—in heaven, with him, for eternity. What a bargain!

The Scripture says, "Every good and perfect gift is from above, coming down from the Father of the heavenly lights, who does not change like shifting shadows" (James 1:17). Acknowledge that the things you have are not yours—they're God's—and be grateful for the honor of "housesitting" for him for a little while.

Visit with the Less Fortunate and Minister to Them

Most of us are not as thankful as we should be because we compare ourselves with those who have more. You can increase your sense of appreciation by spending time with those who are less fortunate. That's another benefit of going on a short-term mission trip. Most people who have visited a Third World country return home thankful to live in the United States where there are smooth roads, safe drinking water, hot showers, ice cubes, air conditioning, etc. Even fast food looks good after a few weeks in another country!

When our boys were younger, we developed a Christmas tradition that taught us something about gratitude. We would buy presents for a needy family and deliver the gifts to them on Christmas Eve. We weren't wealthy by most standards, but Christmas Eve was about the only time my young sons were exposed to people who lived in a crowded trailer park or a dingy downtown apartment.

On the ride home, after several minutes of silence, the boys would begin asking questions about the family we had visited. "Does the father have a job?" "Do they go to church anywhere?" "Did you see the picture of Jesus on the wall?" "Dad, what was it like when you were growing up?" I knew by their questions that they were beginning to understand—not everyone has it as good as we do. For the next several days my sons would exhibit much more gratitude. I wish we had done that sort of thing more often!

My wife and I recently visited a small church in Tennessee while on vacation. We arrived a little early, but we wanted to remain as inconspicuous as possible, so we slid into the third pew and waited for the service to start. Unknown to us, the church only had about thirty members, and they all sat in the back two rows! Essentially, we were in the front row! The young minister delivered a beautiful sermon to those thirty people. I thought to myself, *This guy is a much better preacher than I was at his age*. And I prayed, *Lord, increase his opportunities*. I left realizing how blessed I was to have been led at a young age to a place of ministry where there was fertile soil and good leadership.

The following week I visited a church that at the time was slightly larger than ours, with about fifteen thousand attendees, and I saw that their facilities aren't nearly as nice as ours. I came back home realizing how much God has blessed us. Instead of complaining about the adjacent land we haven't been able to purchase or the traffic problems, I should be on my knees, praying, "O God, forgive me when I whine. I'm blessed indeed."

Avoid like the Plague All Grumbling and Complaining

The Bible makes it clear that God is honored by thanksgiving, but grumbling and griping incur his wrath. For example, even after God had delivered the Israelites from slavery in Egypt and had given them wealth, freedom, water, and manna, they complained constantly. "We miss the fish and melons and cucumbers and onions and garlic we ate in Egypt," they whined. "We want more. We're tired of looking at this manna." The Bible says that the Lord became exceedingly angry because of their grumbling and struck them with a severe plague (see Numbers 11:10, 33).

In 1 Corinthians 10, the apostle Paul warns us to learn

from the negative example of the Israelites in Moses' day. Paul tells us not to be idolaters as some of them were, not to be sexually immoral as some of them were, not to test the Lord as some of them did, "and do not grumble, as some of them did—and were killed by the destroying angel" (1 Corinthians 10:10). Adultery, idol worship, testing God, and grumbling are listed together as horrendous sins that incur the wrath of God.

Some people are specialists at complaining. Think of the things we hear complainers say on a daily basis:

"It's too hot and humid outside."

"It's too cold inside."

"It rains every time I want to do something."

"It's been so dry here lately."

"My husband isn't romantic."

"My wife has no passion."

"My kids won't apply themselves."

"My parents are always interfering."

"My church isn't meeting my needs."

"My Sunday school class is boring."

"My favorite team is pitiful."

The Scripture commands, "Do everything without complaining or arguing, so that you may become blameless and pure, children of God without fault in a crooked and depraved generation, in which you shine like stars in the universe" (Philippians 2:14–15).

Have you developed a habit of complaining? Do you

gripe about every little thing, or about the same thing over and over again? If so, you need to realize that your constant griping is an offense to God, a poor testimony to the lost, and a detriment to your personality. Determine to break your habit. Ask Jesus to transform your personality, and begin today to avoid complaining.

Be Accountable to Someone

A friend told me that when he was younger, kids would taunt a person who complained: "Whiner, whiner, forty-niner!" Ask a family member or close friend to help you cure your habit of grumbling. You can say, "When you catch me complaining, please nudge me, or clear your throat loudly, or say, 'Whiner, whiner, forty-niner!'" I guarantee you, they'll be happy to oblige!

Express Thanks Frequently to God

My mother loves Bill Geiger, who until recently was the minister in my home church—Conneautville Church of Christ—in Conneautville, Pennsylvania. Bill is an excellent preacher and a wonderful person. The church has grown numerically and spiritually under his leadership during the past fifteen years. But he resigned recently to become a part of one of our sister congregations in Louisville, Kentucky, where I live. I immediately sent word to my home church that it was just a coincidence and I didn't have anything to do with it! When they heard Bill was leaving, the church was crushed. My sister Rosanne wrote to me, "Our Camelot is over. Bill resigned yesterday." My mother was so broken up that she could barely talk about it. She cried. It's wonderful to see how she loved her preacher. I wonder why she didn't cry when I left home!

A few weeks after Bill left the church, I called my mother one Sunday night to see how her day had gone. "It was fine," she said. "We had a good day." That's a mature Christian. She easily could have complained about how difficult things are as they struggle to find a new minister. She could have said, "It will just never be the same without Bill here." But she knows that the Bible commands, "Give thanks in all circumstances, for this is God's will for you in Christ Jesus" (1 Thessalonians 5:18).

Count Your Blessings

I read recently that if you own just one Bible, you are abundantly blessed, because a third of the people in the world today do not have access to a Bible. If you can read your Bible, you're more blessed than the two-billion-plus people in the world who cannot read anything at all. If you awoke this morning with more health than illness, you are more blessed than one million people who will not survive the week. If you have never experienced the danger of battle, the loneliness of imprisonment, the agony of torture, or the pangs of starvation, you are more fortunate than 500 million people. If you have food in your refrigerator, clothes on your back, a roof over your head, twenty dollars in your pocket, and a place to sleep, you are richer than 75 percent of the world.

Remember the old song "Count Your Blessings"? There's great advice in those simple words:

> *When upon life's billows you are tempest tossed,*
> *When you are discouraged, thinking all is lost,*
> *Count your many blessings, name them one by one,*
> *And it will surprise you what the Lord hath done!*[1]

Enjoy God's Rich Blessings

In the Book of 1 Timothy, Paul taught the young preacher Timothy how to preach to the rich people in his congregation. He said, "Command those who are rich in this present world not to be arrogant nor to put their hope in wealth, which is so uncertain, but to put their hope in God, who richly provides us with everything *for our enjoyment*" (1 Timothy 6:17). Riches won't save you, Paul warned, so put your hope in God, give away a good portion of what you have, and then *enjoy* the rest because that's why God provided it!

The Bible doesn't say it's wrong to be wealthy. The Bible says it's wrong to be stingy, and it's wrong to be discontented when God has blessed you with much. When your personality is gloomy and melancholy, you're insulting the generous God who has made you rich. But when you enjoy his blessings and seek to be generous to others, God is honored, and your personality attracts others to him.

In the summer of 2000, the city of Louisville hosted the PGA Tournament—one of the three most prestigious and important golf tournaments of the year. (It was the year Tiger Woods beat Bob May in a playoff to win his second consecutive PGA Championship.) I felt honored to have tickets, since the event was sold out. It was nearly impossible to get a parking spot near the golf course, so I expected to have to walk a long way or stand in line for a shuttle. But a few days before the tournament, a man contacted me. "Bob," he said, "I'm Ray Arza. I'm a member of your church. I want you to know that I live two doors down from the main entrance to Valhalla Golf Club. I'm parking cars in my yard the entire week of the PGA Tournament, and I want to offer you a free parking pass for the week." I graciously accepted his offer.

The first day of the tournament, I pulled into his driveway and couldn't believe my good fortune—he was parking cars on his property for twenty dollars a day but wasn't charging me anything! I had my own special spot right near the front of his lot. I got out of my car, and a golf cart picked me up to carry me to the end of his property. I only had to walk a few feet to the main entrance of the golf course. His house was closer to the entrance than the PGA's own VIP lot across the street. It took my son more than an hour to get to the course on a shuttle earlier in the week, so on Sunday afternoon he wised up and rode with me!

Suppose I returned to Ray's house after the first day of the tournament with my shoulders drooped and a sullen look on my face. Ray might say, "Bob, how did it go? Did you enjoy the PGA?"

Suppose I responded, "Oh, I wish I would have just stayed at home. It was too hot. I'm not sure it was worth it. I wish you lived in the first house instead of the second. Some of those people didn't have to walk as far as I did. You know, the golf cart you're using to pick me up doesn't have a top on it. I'm supposed to come back tomorrow. What if it's raining? When I was ready to leave, the golf cart wasn't there to pick me up and drive me back to my car. I was a little disappointed. And you know, Ray, I was hoping you'd have some burgers on the grill in the backyard. I'm hungry and thirsty. I may not come back tomorrow. If I do come back, do you think you could have my name on that spot instead of just a number? That number is too impersonal. But hey, thanks for the spot."

Ray would wonder, *Why did I give a free pass to that guy?* My expression of thanks would be hollow because I refused to enjoy the gift he gave. But if I would come back smiling and say, "Ray, we had a great time! I can't believe we got to park so close! What a thrill!" then he'll think, *I'm glad I was generous.* And I'll be thinking, *Maybe he'll do this again in 2007 when the Ryder Cup is in Louisville!*

God provides many things for our enjoyment. One of the ways we express thanks to him is by living joyful, positive lives.

One of our church members, Mary Frances Myers, died recently. Mary Frances had reason to complain. Severe diabetes had taken most of her eyesight, she was bound to a wheelchair, and she lost her best friend when her husband of more than fifty years died. A few years ago we asked her to give her testimony at a church retreat. I expected her to talk about all the difficult things she had experienced in life and how God had helped her through. Instead, she smiled and said, "I don't have much to say. My testimony is kind of boring! I really love my church, I'm thankful to have been married to a wonderful man for more than fifty years.... Both my children love the Lord and are happily married.... I don't know why God has been so good to me!"

If Mary Frances Myers can endure all of her circumstances and still talk about how good God has been to her, then so can you. It's not about your circumstances, it's about your attitude. With God's help, choose today to change your personality from griping to grateful.

PRAYER **Starter:**

> *Lord, you are a generous Father, and you have made me a rich person. Please forgive me for the times I've complained and failed to be grateful. I am convicted,*

Lord, because I know that every good and perfect gift comes from you. Thank you for your grace most of all, for the indescribable gift of Jesus Christ, and for forgiving my sins—even my sin of ingratitude. Please remind me today through your Holy Spirit—prompt me whenever I complain—and help me to break this habit. I want to be a grateful person and positively impact the people around me so they too might realize and appreciate the blessings you have given us.

DISCUSSION Questions

1. Does a mature Christian always see only the positive or "bright side" of life? Explain.

2. What is your biggest obstacle to gratitude? What do you find yourself complaining about most frequently?

3. Which of the suggested steps in the last section of the chapter do you need to take to become a person of gratitude? How, specifically, will you incorporate these changes?

4. With which leper's excuse for not being grateful do you most closely identify? Give an example of when your attitude reflected one of these excuses. How can you adjust your attitude?

5. Take at least five minutes to list as many things as possible to be thankful for—from small daily blessings to dramatic answers to prayer. Sometime this week, set aside an hour or two and see if you can finish the list!

Better not trouble

trouble till trouble

troubles you, for you

only make your

trouble double trouble

when you do!

—Anonymous

Who of you by worrying can
add a single hour to his life?

—Jesus Christ

FROM worry TO peace

The Worry Company advertised itself as "the world's leading provider of worrying services." "Forget your worries! Your worrying days are over!" they alleged. "Let us worry for you and your friends."

The Worry Company's Web site carried this claim:

Our company is dedicated to lifting the burden of worries from your shoulders. By becoming a member of The Worry Company, you officially transfer all your worries to our highly trained professionals, who will worry for you. Your worries will be declared null and void. They will be entered into our computerized book of worries for a period of one year, and we will worry for you.

P.S. We use only certified worriers.[1]

The second page of their Web site advertised gift items for sale—a certificate of membership for $12.95, mugs for $7.50, a tote bag for $12.95, a golf shirt for $23.95. If you bought all those items, you might have financial worries! I'd be tempted to not pay the bill and let them worry about it!

Don't you wish it were that easy to rid your life of worry?

The next time you were worried about your children or grandchildren, you could e-mail The Worry Company and become carefree. The next time you were churning about financial pressures or job stress, you would just turn it over to The Worry Company and relax! When waiting for lab results from a biopsy, you'd just release your anxiety to a certified worrier and stay cool as a cucumber.

We can smile at the idea of someone else worrying for us, but wouldn't it be great to find a way to be transformed from a person who worries into a person of peace? Jesus Christ really does want to be the Lord of your anxieties. He wants you to cast all your burdens on him and allow him to carry the load for you. Pay attention to what Jesus said in Luke 12 and see how dedicated he is to lifting your burden of worry:

Then Jesus said to his disciples: "Therefore I tell you, do not worry about your life, what you will eat; or about your body, what you will wear. Life is more than food, and the body more than clothes. Consider the ravens: They do not sow or reap, they have no storeroom or barn; yet God feeds them. And how much more valuable you are than birds! Who of you by worrying can add a single hour to his life? Since you cannot do this very little thing, why do you worry about the rest?

"Consider how the lilies grow. They do not labor or spin. Yet I tell you, not even Solomon in all his splendor was dressed like one of these. If that is how God clothes the grass of the field, which is here today, and tomorrow is thrown into the fire, how much more will he clothe you, O you of little faith! And do not set your heart on what you will eat or drink; do not worry about it. For the pagan world runs after all such things, and your Father knows that you need them. But seek his kingdom, and these things will be given to you as well.

"Do not be afraid, little flock, for your Father has been pleased to give you the kingdom. Sell your possessions and give to the poor. Provide purses for yourselves that will not wear out, a treasure in heaven that will not be exhausted, where no thief comes near and no moth destroys. For where your treasure is, there your heart will be also." (Luke 12:22–34)

chapter 2

How often do you worry? For you, is worry just an occasional nervousness that takes the joy out of the day? Or is it more serious—chest pains, dizzy spells, panic attacks, nausea, changes in appetite, withdrawal, insomnia, daily medication? (By the way, if you're a chronic worrier, it's not wrong for you to get help from a qualified medical professional. It may be God's way of beginning some healing for you.)

Do your friends and family worry about you because you worry so much? Do you consider yourself stressed-out much or all of the time? Whether your worries are mild or chronic, Jesus Christ wants to free you of them. He wants to transform you from the inside out. Christ wants your personality to be transformed from panic to peace.

DEFINING THE PROBLEM

Before we discuss how to overcome worry, let's make a distinction between *worry* and *legitimate concern*: *Worry* focuses on improbable difficulties and produces inaction. *Concern* focuses on probable difficulties and produces action.

Legitimate Concern Produces Action

My son Phil has seldom been a worrier. At times, when he was growing up, he was a *cause* of worry! He's always been somewhat fearless and carefree. But now he's the father of a beloved little girl. He said to me recently, "Dad, you ought to get one of those safety mechanisms for your garage door. With grandchildren running around, a garage door can be dangerous if it comes down at the wrong time. For just fifty dollars you can buy a safety eye that prevents it from happening."

I could say, "Phil, you worry about the silliest things." But he had read in the newspaper about someone being injured by a garage door, and he was concerned. Jesus was not telling us we should never buy safety mechanisms for our garage doors or never install smoke alarms, fasten our seat belts, buy life insurance, or save for retirement. Jesus taught us to count the cost of building a tower before we begin, to learn from the ant who works hard and stores up for winter, and to watch the birds who head south when they know cold weather is coming. Often the way to cure our worry is to take some action.

Are you nervous about the upcoming test? Then study!

Are you concerned about your finances? Put yourself on a budget.

Are you anxious about your health? Go to a doctor and follow his or her counsel.

Worry Asks, "What If...?"

With legitimate concerns, proper action can alleviate much of the stress. But anxiety focuses on the improbable, uncontrollable circumstances for which there can be no action. Anxiety is always asking, "What if...?"

You studied for the test, but you worry, "*What if* I forget everything? *What if* I fail?"

You have your finances in order, but you still worry, "*What if* the stock market crashes? *What if* the car breaks down? *What if* the company falters and I get laid off?"

You're in good health, but you still worry, "*What if* I get cancer? *What if* I'm in an accident? *What if* terrorists attack my building?"

Worry focuses on those things you can't control or change. That kind of unproductive behavior is what Jesus wants us to avoid.

THE NEGATIVE EFFECTS OF WORRY

All of God's commands are for our protection and provision. Jesus commands us not to worry for very good reasons.

Worry Impairs Your Personality

My wife used to hate it when I would agree to speak at a national convention, because for several days prior to the event, I worried and fretted and was miserable to be around. When you're constantly worrying, you're no fun to live with! You become somber, critical, negative, withdrawn, and inattentive. Arthur Somers Roche wrote, "Anxiety is a thin stream of fear trickling through the mind. If encouraged, it cuts a channel into which all other thoughts are drained."

Worry Wastes Time and Energy

Worry is like racing your engine when the car is in neutral. You're wasting gasoline, putting unnecessary stress on the motor, and making no progress.

One study showed that the average person's anxiety is focused in the following ways:

- 40 percent on things that will never happen
- 30 percent on things about the past that can't be changed
- 12 percent on other people's opinions that cannot be controlled
- 10 percent about personal health, which only deteriorates with stress
- 8 percent on real problems that will soon be faced

Ninety-two percent of the worrying we do is about things we can't control! What a waste of time!

Pastor John Hagee told about a woman who worried for forty years that she would die of cancer. She died of pneumonia at age seventy. She wasted forty years worrying about the wrong illness!

Corrie ten Boom said, "Worry does not empty tomorrow of its sorrows; it empties today of its strength," How many times I've come to the end of the day and wished I could relive it. I was so worried about something going wrong that I didn't enjoy the day. I wasted it!

Worry Erodes Your Health

Jesus asked, "Who of you by worrying can add a single hour to his life?" (Luke 12:25). Jesus knew that just the opposite is true—worry takes hours away from your life! There are all kinds of stress-related physical ailments—ulcers, heart attacks, high blood pressure, and insomnia, to name a few.

Worry contributes to premature aging. I heard about one anxious father who told his rebellious son, "Every time you act that way, you give me another gray hair!" The boy replied, "Wow, Dad, you must have been a rotten kid—look at Grandpa!"

Think of the drugs that have promised to relieve tension: Valium, Zoloft, Prozac, and many others are designed to calm the nerves. Dr. Rollo May of the Mayo Clinic said, "Tension is one of the most urgent problems of our day. Anxiety is the official emotion of our age."

Worry Harms Your Witness

A doctor told me that before he became a Christian, he and some of his coworkers were turned off to Christianity because of their experiences with Christian ministers. Many of the preachers they treated were terri-

fied of dying. <u>If you're anxious about bad things happen-</u>
<u>ing to you, it's evident to the world that you don't real</u>ly
<u>believe what you say you believe.</u>

Worry Distorts Your Judgment

Distorts Judgment

People can do stupid things when they're under stress.
I read about a man in Indiana who bought a brand-new
sport utility vehicle, then realized after several months
that he was unable to make the payments. He worried
that if he allowed the SUV to be repossessed, his credit
rating would be ruined. Then he had an idea: If he were
to have an accident in which the vehicle was totaled, the
insurance settlement would cover the debt.

The man drove out into the country and found a rarely
traveled road. When he thought no one was looking, he
drove into a tree at thirty-five miles per hour. He got out,
assessed the damage, and realized the vehicle might not
be totaled. So he got back in and ran into the tree again!
Then he telephoned the police.

Thirty minutes later an officer arrived and asked what
had happened. The man explained that he must have
fallen asleep. "That's strange," the officer said. "A farmer
who lives nearby called and said he was watching from a
field when some guy hit a tree, backed up, and then hit it
again. That wouldn't be you, would it?"

The officer warned him that if he tried to turn in the
damage to his insurance company, he'd be arrested for

43

fraud. Now he has payments he can't make on a vehicle he can't drive.

Worry skews your judgment and compounds your problems.

Worry Insults God

The primary reason we worry is that <u>we want to control our own lives rather than trusting God</u> to take care of the future. That's behaving like the pagans who don't know God at all. Jesus calls the person who worries "you of little faith!" (Luke 12:28). <u>When you worry, you're communicating to God that you have no faith in him</u>. You're saying, "I don't believe God will do what he promised he will do." Worry calls God a liar.

God says, "I will provide your every need while you're here on this earth." Worry says, "I'm not sure he will come through."

God says, "When you have problems, I'll make sure you can cope. I won't give you more temptation than you can bear." Worry says, "No way. I won't be able to deal with this."

God says, "Trust me. In the end all things work together for your good." Worry says, "I don't think any good could ever come out of this."

God says, "When the time comes for you to die, I'll take you to be with me." Worry says, "I'm afraid to die, because I'm not sure what will happen to me."

Worry Is a Sin

Now you can understand why the Bible commands us not to worry. Oswald Chambers said that worry is "infidelity" against God because we are communicating that we don't believe God looks after the details of our lives.

In the Luke 12 passage I quoted earlier, Jesus commanded three times, "Do not worry" or "Do not be afraid." When God's Word says, "Do not steal; do not kill; do not bear false witness," you know that to disobey one of those commands would be a sin. Disobeying his command not to worry is also a sin. Worry may be a "respectable" sin among Christians, but it is still a sin.

WORRY CAN BE OVERCOME

You may be saying, "Well, Bob, you don't know me. I'm a worrier, and I'll be a worrier till I die. It's my temperament, and there's nothing I can do about it. I've worried all my life—my mother was a worrier—it's in my genes. You just don't understand my circumstances. If you knew my situation, you'd worry too!"

It's true that some temperaments are more inclined to worry than others. But Jesus never commands us to do something we can't do, and Jesus clearly commanded all of us, "Quit worrying. Don't be anxious."

If you've developed a habit of worrying, you need to go to the Lord and pray, "Father, I confess that I've violated this command. I have a habit of sinning in this way, and chapter **2**

I'm sorry. Please forgive me and help me to overcome this sin by your power."

Acknowledging that God has the power to help you overcome your worry doesn't mean you will never again be tempted to worry. But it does mean that when the temptation arises, you know you can have victory over it through the power of Christ.

Our church has been through two major relocation projects in the last fifteen years. Any preacher will tell you that taking on a building program is one of the most stressful tasks in ministry. The first project was a $7 million new facility about a half-mile down the street from our old building. I worried about it a lot. I worried about fund raising, cost overruns, the criticism of a few members, whether we could maintain the same spirit of excitement and harmony in a different building, whether I could communicate effectively in such a large building, and many other things. It was a very stressful time in my life.

A few years later we decided to relocate again—this time several miles away in a different part of town with the amount of available land we needed. The cost of the new project was $78 million. There were ten times more issues to worry about, but I worried a lot less. I didn't have sleepless nights. I didn't badger the building chairman or the construction manager. I generally enjoyed the entire experience and helped to generate excitement in our congregation about the new building.

There were several reasons I worried less, but two in particular stand out. First, I had gained experience. Much like parents who are more relaxed with their second child, having been through similar circumstances before made me less likely to hit the panic button when stressful situations arose with this project.

The second reason was that I had grown in my faith. I've learned not to worry so much. I knew that a $78 million building project was so big and so far beyond what I could control that I had no option but to turn it over to the Lord. If you can't swim, it doesn't matter if you're in ten feet of water or one hundred feet—you're dead unless you get help. For years, I've been in spiritual territory so far over my head that I know it's a miracle I'm still around. God is working through our church, so I try to step back and let him. But I know that my ability to sleep at night is a testimony that God can help you overcome worry. He helped me. Worry is not inevitable—it's a sin that can be forgiven and overcome.

A PRESCRIPTION FOR OVERCOMING WORRY

When you have your heart set on this world, you're going to worry. If your primary focus is financial security, you will worry because no matter how much money you have, it won't be enough. If your primary focus is your health, you'll worry because you eventually will age and break down, no matter how much oat bran you eat. If your primary focus is your children, you'll worry about their welfare all your life—you can't control them no matter how hard you try.

But if your primary focus is the kingdom of God, everything takes on a different perspective.

A couple of years ago, everybody was worried about the Y2K computer bug. Prophets of doom predicted a national crisis. Electricity and telephone services were destined to crash, they claimed, so experts told us to stockpile water, food, and guns. We worried about something that didn't happen after all and couldn't have been controlled if it did. Today we're still watering our lawns one bottled gallon of Y2K water at a time. If we could have seen the future, we would have disregarded the predictions. We wouldn't have all those gallons of water stored under our basement steps.

God sees the future, and he wants you to get your focus off the physical things of this world and onto spiritual things. It's foolish to give so much attention to a world that is temporary and will soon pass away. Quit worrying about it.

"Do not be afraid, little flock," Jesus says to us, "for your Father has been pleased to give you the kingdom" (Luke 12:32). You have something much more important than the things of this world—you stand to inherit the kingdom of heaven!

Jesus also said, "Seek first his kingdom and his righteousness, and all these things will be given to you as well"

(Matthew 6:33). As C. S. Lewis explained, "Aim at heaven and you get the world thrown in. Aim at the world, and you get neither."

Here are some practical ways you can develop that kind of spiritual focus and allow Jesus to transform you from a worrier into a person of peace.

Become a Christian

If you haven't already done so, make Jesus Christ the Lord and Savior of your life. Cast your sins and your burdens on him. Find a Christian who will baptize you into Christ, and determine that at that point not only your sins but also your worries will be washed away by the blood of Christ.

Jesus invites everyone, "Come to me, all you who are weary and burdened, and I will give you rest. Take my yoke upon you and learn from me, for I am gentle and humble in heart, and you will find rest for your souls. For my yoke is easy and my burden is light" (Matthew 11:28–30). Jesus is the only one truly qualified to carry all our worries.

Worship God Regularly

When you attend your church's worship services each week, it's a regular reminder that God is bigger than your problems. Ruth Bell Graham said, "I've learned that worship and worry cannot live in the same heart. They are mutually exclusive."

chapter **2**

Well-known author Max Lucado is a friend of mine. He told me in a letter about an incident that happened at his church in San Antonio on Easter Sunday:

I typically sit on the front row. From the row behind me I heard the sweet voice of a young boy. "What is that, Daddy?" he whispered.

The father's voice was deep and kind. "These are crackers. They help us think about Jesus' death on the cross."

I chuckled at his impossible assignment—explaining the Lord's Supper to a child. The questions continued with the cup of juice. "What is that, Daddy?"

"It's grape juice. It reminds us of the blood of Jesus," the father began. Then he went on to, as best he could, explain the symbol.

After a few moments, I turned, both to see who the father was and to give him a knowing smile. As it turned out, the father was David Robinson. On his lap was six-year-old David Jr.

Only the night before, David had led the San Antonio Spurs to a playoff victory over the Phoenix Suns. Within twenty-four hours he would be in Arizona trying to do it again. Both games would be broadcast on national television, seen by millions.

But David would be the first to tell you: Neither contest compared to the precious moments he had with his son on Easter Sunday. Years from now, long after the headlines have faded and the games have been forgotten, it will not matter who won or lost on the court. What will matter is that this young boy had a daddy who told him about Jesus Christ.

David Robinson could have skipped church that day to stay home and prepare for the next game. He could have been so preoccupied with all the stress and pressure and demands of competition that he gave short, impatient answers to his young son's questions. Instead, Robinson can handle graciously the stress of performing at the highest level of professional sports specifically because he worships God regularly. And I imagine his son will have an easier time facing his own worries because of the example his dad has set for him. The psalmist wrote, "Though an army besiege me, my heart will not fear; though war break out against me, even then will I be confident. One thing I ask of the LORD, this is what I seek: that I may dwell in the house of the LORD all the days of my life, to gaze upon the beauty of the LORD and to seek him in his temple" (Psalm 27:3–4).

Trust the Providence of God

Jesus said, "Consider the ravens." Ravens are nasty birds. They're scavengers, feeding primarily on dead animals. Nobody wants ravens around. "Yet," Jesus said, chapter **2**

"God feeds them. And how much more valuable you are than birds!" (Luke 12:24).

The raven doesn't pace his limb at night worrying, "I wonder if there will be any road kill tomorrow. What's the weather report?" You can watch the animal channel for months, and I guarantee they won't show you a raven's nest with a storage shed attached. Yet the raven has enough to eat every day. Conversely there's no such thing as an anorexic raven that refuses to eat, worrying about how trim its body appears. If God cares for the least of these creatures, won't he see to it that you're cared for?

Jesus also said, "Consider how the lilies grow." My father-in-law grew hundreds of rosebushes. My wife has transplanted about a dozen of them in our backyard. I've learned that roses require a lot of attention—they have to be pruned, fertilized, and covered for protection from the frost.

You don't have to protect lilies. They thrive in the wild in Palestine—they need no attention, no cultivation, no overseer—and yet these beautiful flowers will grow to cover a hillside. I like the way *The Message* paraphrases Jesus' description of the lilies in Luke 12:27: "Have you ever seen color and design quite like it? The ten best-dressed men and women in the country look shabby alongside them."

"If that is how God clothes the grass of the field," Jesus continued, "which is here today, and tomorrow is thrown into the fire, how much more will he clothe you, O you of little faith" (Luke 12:28).

How much evidence do you need before you're convinced that God is taking care of you? How many meals will you have to eat before you say, "I trust I'm going to have enough to eat every day of my life, so I'll quit worrying about food"? How many articles of clothing will you have to hang in your closet before you say, "God is providing me with enough to wear"? How many nights will you go to bed with a roof over your head and a secure place to sleep before you conclude, "God is going to protect me and provide for me"? How many prayers must be answered before you reason, "God is watching out for me"? How much stuff will you have to accumulate before you decide, "I'm content—God has blessed me with enough; I don't need any more"?

Face Reality

Consider the birds. They don't worry, but they're not without their problems. They have to fly south for hundreds of miles in order to survive the winter. Their eggs may be eaten by snakes or other predators. They age and die.

Consider the lilies. They're beautiful, but what happens to them? They wilt, get cut down, and are thrown into the fire.

Trusting in the providence of God doesn't mean ignoring reality. People die. Kids have accidents and sometimes even get killed. Stocks plunge. Companies go bankrupt. Couples get divorced.

Some people will tell you that the best way to overcome worry is to put it out of your mind. "Just don't think about it," they'll say. But you can't do that for long. The best way to overcome worry is to face the truth: You will have trouble in this world. But God will enable you to get through it.

Jesus said, "I have told you these things, so that in me you may have peace. In this world you will have trouble. But take heart! I have overcome the world" (John 16:33).

Paul wrote from a prison cell, "I know what it is to be in need, and I know what it is to have plenty. I have learned the secret of being content in any and every situation, whether well fed or hungry, whether living in plenty or in want. I can do everything through him who gives me strength" (Philippians 4:12–13).

The providence of God is not shallow. Jesus didn't say, "Nothing bad is ever going to happen to you; everything is going to be fine, so quit worrying." If you think nothing really bad is going to happen to you, your peace is unrealistic and temporary. You're going to be devastated when hard times hit—and they will hit. God's providence doesn't mean nothing bad will happen to you, but it does mean that God will reinforce and strengthen you through whatever tragedy you face. The Scripture promises, "God is faithful; he will not let you be tempted beyond what you can bear.

But when you are tempted, he will also provide a way out so that you can stand up under it" (1 Corinthians 10:13).

When Corrie ten Boom was in her late teens, she witnessed Nazi soldiers arrest and torture an older Christian. She said to her dad, "I couldn't stand that. I would wilt under persecution. I'm afraid I wouldn't be faithful."

Her father said, "Corrie, God will give you the faith you need."

But she kept insisting, "I don't have that kind of courage and faith."

Finally her dad said, "Do you remember when you were a little girl and we took rides on the train? I kept your ticket in my pocket. Do you remember when I gave you your ticket?"

She said, "Yes, just before I got on the train."

"Right," said her father. "I kept it until you needed it so you wouldn't lose it. God will give you the faith you need. He will empower you by his Holy Spirit according to your need. Trust him for that."

When Corrie ten Boom was later arrested and persecuted, her faithfulness became an inspiration to all Christians.

Trusting God's providence means believing that whatever happens—even persecution or death—God will see you through.

When John Brownfield, who attended our church, learned that he had inoperable cancer, he was determined to be faithful. He later told me, "I used to wonder if I could cope with news like this. But I've been surprised at how simple it is. It's just a matter of faith. I know I'm going to a better place. I really do have a peace that passes understanding."

We were on a church golf trip at the time, and John Brownfield went out right after talking to me and shot a thirty-seven on the front nine—an excellent score! On the last day of the trip, John was paired with a young man from Illinois who was not a Christian. The young man asked John a lot of questions about his illness and faith. John's peace in spite of physical adversity had a greater impact on that young man than any tracts he could have shared.

David wrote, "The LORD is my shepherd; I shall not want.... Yea, though I walk through the valley of the shadow of death, I will fear no evil: for thou art with me; thy rod and thy staff they comfort me" (Psalm 23:1, 4 KJV).

Review God's Promises

The Scriptures are filled with promises from God. Here's a sampling:

- Be strong and courageous. Do not be afraid or terrified because of them, for the LORD your God goes with you; he will never leave you nor forsake you. (Deuteronomy 31:6)

- Cast your cares on the LORD and he will sustain you; he will never let the righteous fall. (Psalm 55:22)

- For the LORD God is a sun and shield; the LORD bestows favor and honor; no good thing does he withhold from those whose walk is blameless. (Psalm 84:11)

- But now, this is what the LORD says—he who created you, O Jacob, he who formed you, O Israel: "Fear not, for I have redeemed you; I have summoned you by name; you are mine. When you pass through the waters, I will be with you; and when you pass through the rivers, they will not sweep over you. When you walk through the fire, you will not be burned; the flames will not set you ablaze." (Isaiah 43:1–2)

- I, even I, am he who blots out your transgressions, for my own sake, and remembers your sins no more. (Isaiah 43:25)

- If you remain in me and my words remain in you, ask whatever you wish, and it will be given you. (John 15:7)

- Believe in the Lord Jesus, and you will be saved— you and your household. (Acts 16:31)

- And my God will meet all your needs according to his glorious riches in Christ Jesus. (Philippians 4:19)

- Come near to God and he will come near to you. (James 4:8)

- If we confess our sins, he is faithful and just and will forgive us our sins and purify us from all unrighteousness. (1 John 1:9)

Write some of those promises down. Review them. Memorize them. Ask yourself, *Do I really believe what I say I believe?* If so, then act like it.

Years ago some Native American tribes had a peculiar rite of passage when a boy reached the age of thirteen. The boy was blindfolded, led out into the woods, and left to spend the night alone. His courage would be proven if he could sit and listen to the frightening sounds of the night without removing the blindfold.

When he felt the warmth of the morning sun, he was allowed to remove the blindfold—to find that his father was sitting just a few feet away. Unknown to the boy, his father had been by his side throughout the night, watching over him and protecting him from any real danger.

You may go through some terrifying times. But God's Word assures us that our Father never forsakes us. The writer of Hebrews reminds us, "God has said, 'Never will I leave you; never will I forsake you.' So we say with confidence, 'The Lord is my helper; I will not be afraid. What can man do to me?'" (Hebrews 13:5–6).

The Bible promises, "He will not let your foot slip—he who watches over you will not slumber; indeed, he who watches over Israel will neither slumber nor sleep. The LORD watches over you—the LORD is your shade at your right hand" (Psalm 121:3–5).

Lay Up Treasures in Heaven

After Jesus gave the command not to worry, he gave this prescription for overcoming anxiety and developing a spiritual perspective: "Sell your possessions and give to the poor. Provide purses for yourselves that will not wear out, a treasure in heaven that will not be exhausted, where no thief comes near and no moth destroys. For where your treasure is, there your heart will be also" (Luke 12:33–34).

I mentioned earlier that my father-in-law loved roses. He had more than three hundred rose bushes at one time, and he was president of the local Rose Society. People would come from the surrounding area just to look at Virgil Thomas's rose garden. Virgil passed away several months ago at the age of ninety. At his funeral several people made reference to roses, and a number of roses were arranged on the casket. My daughter-in-law Kellie sang a most appropriate song—"Where the Roses Never Fade":

> I am going to a city
> Where the streets with gold are laid,
> Where the tree of life is blooming,
> And the roses never fade.

59

chapter 2

Here they bloom but for a season,
Soon their beauty is decayed;
I am going to a city
Where the roses never fade.[2]

God commands us to give, not because he needs it or the church needs it or the poor need it. Those are secondary reasons. We give of our possessions primarily because of *our* need. I heard about a missionary who visited the office of a shipping magnate to ask for a donation. The wealthy Christian businessman complied and wrote a check for a generous amount. Just as he handed the check to the missionary, the businessman received an emergency call informing him that one of his barges had met disaster and had sunk, destroying all of the cargo on board.

The owner asked the missionary to return the check so he could write another. The missionary assumed that because of the disaster the man didn't feel he could give so generously. But the owner tore up the check and wrote another for twice the amount. When the missionary asked why he was doubling his gift, the businessman said, "That call was a reminder from my Father not to put my hopes in the cargo of this world."

One of the surest ways to stop worrying is to give more. When we give generously, we're reminded that our trust is not in the things of this world. We need to remember that the things of this earth will fade away but that we are headed for "a city where the roses never fade."

Learn the Art of Living One Day at a Time

The birds go to sleep at night depending on God to provide for their needs. The flowers are here today and gone tomorrow, and you will be too. "Therefore," Jesus said, "do not worry about tomorrow, for tomorrow will worry about itself. Each day has enough trouble of its own" (Matthew 6:34).

Shortly after the terrorist attacks of September 11, 2001, I remembered an interview I once heard with several people who had lived in London during World War II and survived the daily German bombings during the Blitz. In the interview, they each were asked about their favorite period of life. I was surprised when nearly every one of them pinpointed World War II as being the happiest time of their lives. They said, "There's something about living under the threat of death that helps you appreciate every day."

We're writing this book at a time when people in America are worried about Anthrax attacks, war in Afghanistan, a shaky stock market, and an uncertain future. For Americans, there's a sense in which these are the worst of times since World War II. But in another sense, it's the best of times. There never has been a time when the country was more united, more patriotic, or more open to the gospel of Jesus Christ. Now more than ever, people realize that the future is uncertain. That realization leads us to think about spiritual things and to treasure each day.

The *Los Angeles Times* reprinted the following essay by Ann Wells that illustrates the importance of living life one day at a time:

My brother-in-law opened the bottom drawer of my sister's bureau and lifted out a tissue-wrapped package. He discarded the tissue and handed me the slip. It was exquisite; silk, hand-made and trimmed with a cobweb of lace. The price tag with an astronomical figure on it was still attached.

"Jan bought this the first time we went to New York at least 8 or 9 years ago. She never wore it. She was saving it for a special occasion."

He took the slip from me and put it on the bed with the other clothes we were taking to the mortician. His hands lingered on the soft material for a moment, then he slammed the drawer shut and turned to me.

"Don't ever save anything for a special occasion. Every day you are alive is a special occasion."

I remembered those words through the funeral and the days that followed when I helped him and my niece attend to all the sad chores that follow an unexpected death. I'm still thinking about those words, and they've changed my life.... I'm not saving anything.... We use our good china and crystal for every special event; such as losing a pound, getting the sink unstopped, the first camellia blossom.... "Someday" and "one of these days" are losing their grip on my vocabulary. If it's worth seeing or hearing or doing, I want to see and hear and do it now.... I'm trying not to put off, hold back, or save anything that would add laugher and luster to our lives. And every morning when I open my eyes, I tell myself that it is special.[3]

Yesterday is gone. Tomorrow is not assured. You have the privilege of living this day. Soak it up. Enjoy life to the fullest. The psalmist wrote, "This is the day the LORD has made; let us rejoice and be glad in it" (Psalm 118:24).

The Bible promises that God "will keep in perfect peace him whose mind is steadfast" because he trusts in the Lord (Isaiah 26:3). "Do not be anxious about anything, but in everything, by prayer and petition, with thanksgiving, present your requests to God. And the peace of God, which transcends all understanding, will guard your hearts and your minds in Christ Jesus" (Philippians 4:6–7).

If you want to have a positive impact on the lives of people around you, if you want to be fun to live with, if you want an attitude adjustment, let Jesus Christ transform you from a worrier into someone who possesses the peace that passes understanding.

PRAYER **Starter:**

Lord, you are a big God! I believe your ability to take care of my problems today. Please forgive me for the times I've sinned by worrying. Help me remember that nothing will happen today that you and I can't handle together. You have given me this day. Help me to live it to the fullest, to enjoy today's blessings, and to trust in your promises. Calm my anxious heart and fill me with the peace that passes understanding. Help that peace to overflow to those around me. Your love endures forever, and your faithfulness throughout all generations!

DISCUSSION **Questions**

1. On a scale of one to ten, how much do you worry? What do you worry about most?

2. Why do we find it difficult to take our burdens to the Lord and leave them there?

3. Who among your acquaintances seems to trust God the most? What characteristics indicate this trust? Do you believe God can transform your attitude from worry to peace?

4. What helps you overcome worry? Which of the practical steps listed in this chapter do you most need to take?

5. Which of God's promises is your favorite? Which is the hardest for you to believe?

Forgiveness

will set

you free.

—Mother Teresa

Forgive, and you will
be forgiven.

—Jesus Christ

chapter 3

FROM bitterness TO forgiveness

At long last Jane Graafschap and her husband, Ralph, had brought their children through the crazy maze of adolescence. Now the kids were graduated and gone, and Jane was glad. Finally she would have a life of her own and make something of herself.

In his book *Forgive and Forget*, Lewis Smedes recounts how a family tragedy interrupted Jane's plans. Ralph's younger brother and his wife were killed in an automobile accident. They left behind three children—ages eight, ten, and twelve. Ralph felt it was his duty to take care of his brother's orphaned children, so the kids moved in with them.

chapter 3

But Ralph's job required him to be on the road a lot. Nine years dragged by as Jane longed for an empty nest again. Two of the kids went on to college. Now only the youngest, a seventeen-year-old boy, was at home. In just a few months, Jane thought, she and Ralph would be home free. But not quite.

As the years passed, Ralph found Jane less attractive. His secretary Sue, however, was a dazzler who really knew how to boost his ego. Ralph and Sue became convinced that their "love" for each other was too true to be denied and too powerful to be resisted, so Ralph divorced Jane and married Sue. The new couple's happiness was reaffirmed by an "accepting" church that celebrated their newfound joy with them.

"But Ralph needed one more stroke of acceptance," Smedes writes. "So he called Jane and asked her to forgive him and be glad with him that he was finally a happy man. 'I want you to bless me,' he said."[1]

Jane told Ralph in very graphic terms where he could go.

What? Forgive? Throw away the only power she had—the strength of her hate? Her contempt was her power, her dignity, her self-esteem. It was unfair to ask her to forgive. The least the louse deserved was the steady stream of her scorn.

…There is a lot to be said for not forgiving people who have done us wrong. Why should people cut and thrust their way through our lives, leaving us bleeding in their wake, and then expect us to forgive everything and act as if nothing went wrong? Forgiving is an outrage against...dues-paying morality.[2]

Maybe you've gone through a bitter divorce, a church split, an awkward breakup of a family business, or a fight over the settling of an estate. You've been negatively impacted for a long time, and the last thing you want to do is forgive. You're right—they don't deserve to be forgiven.

But I have news for you. Your unwillingness to forgive is not hurting the person who deserves to be hurt. It's destroying you. Few emotions can destroy your personality like bitterness. An unforgiving spirit makes you vengeful, calloused, guarded, joyless, and depressed.

The Bible says, "See to it that no one misses the grace of God and that no bitter root grows up to cause trouble and defile many" (Hebrews 12:15). Your refusal to forgive will cause a bitter root to grow, and that bitterness will not only cause trouble for you but will also defile many around you. Your desire for revenge cancels out the grace of God. Bitterness is like acid. It does more damage to the container in which it is stored than the object on which it is poured.

When Jesus taught us how to pray, he included in the middle of the Lord's prayer this phrase: "Forgive us our

sins, for we also forgive everyone who sins against us"
(Luke 11:4). We like the first part of that prayer—forgive
us our sins. We know we need it! But the second part is
tough—forgive *everyone* who sins against us? Jesus made it
clear that if we really understand how much of a debt God
has forgiven, we'll automatically be gracious to those who
owe us.

For you, this chapter may be the most important one
in this book. Jesus Christ cannot transform you until
you're ready to let go of your bitterness. If you're holding a
grudge against even one person, that bitterness will sour
your entire personality.

Christ has the power to change you—if you're willing to
let him. Mother Teresa said, "Forgiveness will set you free."
Few actions can transform your personality as quickly and
dramatically as the decision to release the bitterness you
harbor in your heart. Let God's Word sink deep into your
soul, and let him transform your spirit as you read this
chapter. May Jesus teach you to pray, every day, "Forgive
our sins as we forgive everyone who sins against us."

YOU HAVE BEEN FORGIVEN MUCH

A key to forgiving those who have wronged you is
grasping the first part of the forgiveness prayer—"forgive
our sins." When you realize how much you've been forgiven, it becomes easier to forgive those who have sinned
against you.

You Have Violated God's Laws

If you break man's law, you owe a debt to the government. If you speed, evade paying income tax, sell drugs, or murder someone, you can be fined, imprisoned, or even executed. We speak of "paying one's debt to society."

You owe a huge debt to God. This is God's world, and God has established certain laws by which you are to live. When you break those laws (and we all have), you owe a debt to him that must be paid. His Word says, "The wages of sin is death" (Romans 6:23).

The Bible mentions a lot of ways we violate God's laws, and each violation carries a severe penalty. Consider the following four categories of sins, and you'll begin to realize how much you've been forgiven.

Sins of Commission

These are the outward sins—the ones we usually picture when we talk about breaking one of God's commands. David deliberately brought Bathsheba into his home and committed adultery with her. Judas, with malice and forethought, plotted to betray Jesus. When someone deliberately lies, steals, kills, or commits adultery, he is guilty of *committing* a sin—thus the term "sin of commission."

Sins of Stumbling

James wrote, "For whoever keeps the whole law and yet stumbles at just one point is guilty of breaking all of it"

(James 2:10). On the night Jesus was arrested, Simon Peter committed this type of sin. He didn't plan to deny Jesus—just the opposite. He swore he would never deny his Lord. But in the heat of the moment, when Peter was accused of being Jesus' disciple, he blurted out, "I don't know the man!" You can probably think of some times you've committed a sin of stumbling—you get startled by a near miss on the freeway and a swear word escapes your lips; you get angry and retaliate; you get careless and gossip. You didn't mean to let it happen, but in the heat of the moment, you stumbled and sinned.

Sins of Omission

These are the things you know you should have done, but you neglected to do them. You should have written that thank-you note; you should have given money to that missionary; you should have taken time to encourage your wife; you should have told that man about Jesus; you should have gotten out of bed and gone to church. Is it a sin when you don't do something you know you should have done? The standard of righteousness is set very high by a perfect, holy God. His Word says, "Anyone, then, who knows the good he ought to do and doesn't do it, sins" (James 4:17).

Sins of Imagination

The people of Noah's day were judged because the thoughts of their hearts were always evil (see Genesis 6:5).

Jesus said, "You've heard it said, 'Don't murder,' but I say to you, 'Don't be angry with your brother.' You've heard it said, 'Do not commit adultery,' but I say to you, 'Do not lust in your heart'" (Matthew 5:21–22, 27–28, paraphrased). The psalmist wrote, "The LORD knows the thoughts of man; he knows that they are futile" (Psalm 94:11).

If all your thoughts were written down in a book and published, you'd buy every copy so nobody could read it! How big a book would it take to write down all the sinful *thoughts* you've had? Would it have to be a library? Just for this month's thoughts?

By now you're probably saying, "Thanks, Bob. Now I feel like a rotten person." That's the point.

One of the Greek words in the New Testament for sin is *hamartia*. In the classical Greek language, an archer missing his target was said to have committed *hamartia*. He had missed the mark.[3] The Bible commands us to be perfect as our heavenly Father is perfect (see Matthew 5:48). Any time you fall short of that ideal, you miss the mark—you sin.

Let's illustrate it this way: How many times a day do you think you sin? You have lustful thoughts, you act selfishly, you neglect to show compassion to your child. A fairly good person may sin only thirty or forty times a day. Even a saint probably sins ten times a day. But let's give you the benefit of the doubt. We'll say you're a super-saint, and you sin only three times a day. Only three times in a normal day do you commit an act of disobedience, have a lustful thought, neglect to do what you know is right, or do the right thing with the wrong motivation. That means you sin 1,095 times a year. That's an extremely conservative estimate, don't forget. If you live to be seventy, you will have committed more than seventy-six thousand sins!

Don't forget that just one sin is all you need to be condemned. But you've accumulated seventy-six thousand! Not all of them are "little" sins, either. Among those seventy-six thousand are some biggies. What are some of yours? Adultery, stealing, abortion, profanity, blasphemy, drunkenness?

How would you like to stand before the Holy God of the universe with seventy-six thousand counts against you? Over the years, you've accumulated a huge debt against God!

God Offers Forgiveness

Even as gigantic as that debt is, God offers to cancel it through Jesus Christ. "For God so loved the world that he gave his one and only Son, that whoever believes in him shall not perish but have eternal life" (John 3:16). Instead of making you pay the debt for your sin, he paid it for you. God came to earth as a human being in the form of his son, Jesus Christ, and he allowed himself to be tortured and crucified as a payment for your sin. "God made him who had no sin to be sin for us, so that in him we might become the righteousness of God" (2 Corinthians 5:21).

When Jesus Christ died on the cross, the sins of the world were heaped on him. He became guilty of all one million of my sins. That's why the sun turned black, God turned his back, and Jesus cried out, "My God, my God, why have you forsaken me?" (Matthew 27:46). God "laid on him the iniquity of us all" (Isaiah 53:6).

But just before he died, Jesus said, "*Tetelestai,*" which is translated "It is finished." It can also mean "Paid in full." The debt of sin is paid. Canceled. Deleted.

> You see, at just the right time, when we were still powerless, Christ died for the ungodly. Very rarely will anyone die for a righteous man, though for a good man someone might possibly dare to die. But God demonstrates his own love for us in this: While we were still sinners, Christ died for us. Since we have now been justified by his blood, how much more shall we be saved from God's wrath through him! (Romans 5:6–9)

> *Jesus paid it all;*
> *All to Him I owe;*
> *Sin had left a crimson stain;*
> *He washed it white as snow.* [4]

God's Grace Covers Past, Present, and *Future* Sins!

Romans 6:23 says, "The wages of sin is death, but the gift of God is eternal life in Christ Jesus our Lord." When you became a Christian, you accepted that gift. When you were baptized, it was a reminder that all of your sins were washed away by the blood of Christ.

You probably don't have any trouble believing that Christ washed away the sins you committed before you became a Christian. But have you lived a perfect life since that day you accepted Christ? Have you even lived a perfect life in the last twenty-four hours? I doubt it!

You've probably struggled with feelings of guilt over how many times you've let Christ down since you gave him your heart. Here's the good news: Jesus doesn't just forgive your past sins, he offers to forgive your present and future sins as well!

The Book of 1 John is addressed to fellow believers in Christ, yet John writes, "If we claim to be without sin, we deceive ourselves and the truth is not in us. If we confess our sins, he is faithful and just and will forgive us our sins and purify us from all unrighteousness" (1 John 1:8–9). Did you catch that? God is faithful and just. You always thought of God's justice bringing punishment, right? But John tells us that God's justice for you means forgiveness of *all* your sins—past, present, and future—because Jesus has already paid the debt in advance!

A few years ago my wife and I were on vacation in Gatlinburg, Tennessee, and visited one of our favorite restaurants, The Peddler. It's a great place to eat, but it's not cheap. After we finished eating and had waited a while for the check, I finally asked the waiter, "Can we please have our bill?"

He smiled and said, "It has been taken care of."

"Who did that?" I asked.

The waiter pointed to a couple across the room whom I barely recognized and answered, "They took care of your meal."

When we walked over to thank them, they said, "We're new members at Southeast and just wanted to tell you thanks because the church means so much to us."

The waiter would have been dishonest to charge me for that meal. If he had made me pay, he would have been unjust. It had already been paid in full.

Every sin you've ever committed and every sin you ever will commit has been paid in advance and in full by Jesus Christ. It would be dishonest—unjust—for God to make you pay for your sins when Jesus already has paid the price. That's why Paul said God is faithful *and just* to forgive you and cleanse you from all unrighteousness!

Does that mean we're free to sin all we want? Not quite. I was tempted to ask our friends at The Peddler, "Where are you eating tomorrow night?" But out of respect for the sacrifice they had made, I didn't do that. If you think God's free gift means you can go out and sin as much as you want, then you don't appreciate the extreme sacrifice God made to save you from sin, and you don't understand the harmful consequences of sin from which

God wants to save you (see Romans 6). When you under-stand what God has done to save you from sin, you'll feel compelled to live as righteously as possible out of grati-tude for the freedom you've been given.

I like the third stanza of the hymn "It Is Well with My Soul":

> My sin, Oh the bliss of this glorious tho't:
> My sin, not in part but the whole,
> Is nail'd to the cross, and I bear it no more,
> Praise the Lord, praise the Lord, O my soul![5]

GOD EXPECTS YOU TO FORGIVE OTHERS

Jesus taught us to pray, "Forgive our sins in the same way we have forgiven others." "Forgive our trespasses," some translations say, "as we forgive those who trespass against us." I heard about one little boy who prayed, "Forgive us our trash baskets as we forgive those who put trash in our baskets!" Jesus knew we would have debtors—people who put trash in our baskets. There will be people who dump on you and who owe you a debt they can never repay.

Maybe a drunk driver slammed into your car or the car of one you loved and your life will never be the same. Perhaps a family member borrowed money from you and didn't keep his promise to repay or cheated you in the settling of an estate. Maybe a former spouse left you alone, financially strapped, and emotionally broken. An employee might have embezzled money from you, or perhaps a boss didn't fulfill her promises and left you unemployed. Maybe your minister wounded you and never attempted to make things right.

Doesn't the phrase "Forgive us our debts as we forgive our debtors" frighten you a little? I want God to forgive me like *God* forgives, not like *I forgive*!

Following the Lord's Prayer, Jesus expounded on this forgiveness theme: "For if you forgive men when they sin against you, your heavenly Father will also forgive you. But if you do not forgive men their sins, your Father will not forgive your sins" (Matthew 6:14–15). What did Jesus mean?

John Stott explained, "This certainly does not mean that our forgiveness of others earns us the right to be forgiven. It is rather that God forgives only the penitent, and that one of the chief evidences of true penitence is a forgiving spirit."[6]

Years ago I watched one of my sons play on the school basketball team. He started the game and played well, but then the coach took him out and never put him back in. I left the event churning about how my son was treated unfairly. As I was driving away, my anger toward the coach was building. *He's made it clear that he doesn't like our church*, I reminded myself. *I know he doesn't like me, and*

he's taking it out on my son. My son is at a vulnerable age. He
needs to be boosted up, and that coach is tearing him down. I
vowed I'd never be an interfering father, but I'm going to give
him a piece of my mind!

I looked at the clock and realized it was the time of day
when my sermons are broadcast on one of the local radio
stations. I tuned in to hear which sermon was being aired.
It was one about forgiveness! I listened as my own voice
preached to me, paraphrasing Jesus' parable in Matthew 18:

> A servant owed the king $20 million. The king, realiz-
> ing the man could never repay the debt, forgave him the
> entire debt. But then that forgiven servant went out and
> found a man who owed him twenty dollars. When his
> debtor couldn't pay, he threw him into prison. When
> the king discovered what the ungrateful servant had
> done, he was furious and threw the man in prison,
> promising to make him pay every dime.

"If we want God to forgive us our huge debt of sin," I
concluded, "then we have to be willing to forgive those
who wound us."

I turned off the radio. I didn't want to hear any more.
It made me mad! I decided that day that it's better to listen to music than preaching while you're driving a car!

When you understand how much God has forgiven
you, then you know it is essential for you to forgive others. A spirit of submission to Christ cannot reside in the

same place as a spirit of bitterness. One of the two will be edged out. Followers of Christ must forgive their debtors.

Max Lucado wonders if many of us are spending our lives trying to collect the bills someone owes us. Someone owes us an apology, a second chance, a fresh start, an explanation, a thank you, a childhood, a marriage. Lucado writes, "You can spend the rest of your life demanding payment, collecting bills, or you can say, 'This is no way to live. I'm going on to other things.'"[7] What are you going to do with those indebted to you? Will you keep carrying your bitterness, or will you determine to forgive?

THE FOUR STAGES OF FORGIVENESS

If you want to extend genuine forgiveness, remember that forgiveness is a process that takes time and energy. It would be nice if forgiveness were a one-time event: You forgive a person, and it's over—forgotten—and the relationship is restored. But in reality, forgiveness takes time. A huge debt is usually repaid on an installment plan.

According to author Lewis Smedes, we encounter four stages on our way to forgiveness.[8]

Hurt

Hurt begins the first stage. Smedes wrote, "When somebody causes you pain so deep and unfair that you cannot forget it, you are pushed into the first stage of the crisis of forgiveness." People might think that since you're a Christian, you shouldn't be so easily wounded. But you still hurt. You weep. You may even pound your fist into a wall. You can't sleep for the pain. You might even gripe to those close to you about the wrong you've suffered.

Anger

Anger usually is the second stage. Smedes explains that in this stage you can't shake the memory, and you can't bring yourself to wish your enemy well. Sometimes you wish the person who hurt you could suffer the way you've had to suffer, and you even think of some ways to make it happen. I heard about a classified advertisement that read, "For sale: Wedding dress. Never worn. Will trade for .38 special."

In this second stage, your sense of justice has been wounded. It's not fair that you're still hurting, and it hurts worse than you thought it would. You're angry, and you dream of ways to get even—you write a nasty letter and think about sending it; you imagine telling his friends what a louse he is; at the very least, you pout and refuse to speak to him in the hopes that he'll sense how you feel.

You might think a Christian shouldn't feel this way. The Bible says, "'In your anger do not sin': Do not let the sun go down while you are still angry, and do not give the devil a foothold" (Ephesians 4:26–27). It's not wrong to be angry. In fact, when people try to bury the fact that they're angry and have been treated unjustly, they often cover over a festering wound that may never heal. The goal is to deal properly with your anger—to place the blame squarely where it belongs, to admit that you were treated unfairly, and then to choose forgiveness instead of bitterness.

Healing

Healing comes next for the person who chooses to forgive. If you have a flesh wound, the pain slowly goes away, and in a few weeks the body heals itself. The more serious the wound, the longer the healing process takes. The same is true with emotional wounds. Eventually, they heal. If your wound is serious enough, an emotional scar may remain. But healing can come. Some emotional wounds can be so deep that you need the help of a counselor or pastor to properly "clean" the wound so healing can begin. But the day will come when you can genuinely smile and laugh again because you've been freed by forgiveness.

Restoration

Restoration concludes the forgiveness process. Smedes explains that at this stage "you invite the person who hurt you back into your life. Love can move you both toward a new and restored relationship. The fourth stage depends on the person you forgive as much as it depends on you." Reconciliation is facilitated by the repentance, remorse, and

Reconciliation

Repent. Remorse Honesty

honesty of the perpetrator. He or she may not repent, in which case you are left to heal alone. Or the offense may be so serious that trust has been broken, and it would be unwise to completely restore the relationship. (We'll talk more about this later in the chapter.) But regardless of whether complete restoration occurs, any willing person, with God's help, can reach the place where healing occurs and appropriate steps of restoration become possible.

THE QUALIFIERS OF FORGIVENESS

I recently told our congregation the story you read at the beginning of this chapter about Ralph running off with the secretary and leaving Jane behind. In the sermon I implied that Jane should forgive Ralph. Some people left angry with me that day. *How could she be expected to forgive him?* they wondered. Forgiveness is never easy, but perhaps one reason some people had such difficulty with my implication is that they misunderstood what forgiveness means. Forgiveness has some important qualifiers.

Forgiveness Does Not Mean Endorsement of the Behavior

When you forgive someone, you're not saying that what they did was right. You're not saying it didn't hurt. Just the opposite—when you forgive, you're confirming that what they did *was* wrong and *did* hurt, or else they wouldn't need to be forgiven! Forgiveness simply means releasing your right to retaliate. Like Jesus, you choose to absorb the pain yourself rather than seek vengeance.

Forgiveness Does Not Mean Exemption from Judgment

One of the reasons people have trouble forgiving is that it goes counter to our instinctive need for justice. "You mean, I have to forgive the bum and let him go free, and he's going to get away with what he did to me?" you may ask. Forgiveness doesn't mean you must stand in the way of justice. Romans 12:19 says, "Do not take revenge, my friends, but leave room for God's wrath, for it is written: 'It is mine to avenge; I will repay,' says the Lord." Sometimes the governing authorities take care of justice. Sometimes justice won't be served until eternity. Forgiveness means you won't seek justice on your own terms. You won't act as judge and jury; you won't try to play God. Instead, you'll release your right to get even and leave justice to God.

Forgiveness Does Not Mean Restoration of Trust

There is a difference between forgiving a person and trusting him or her. Forgiveness can be instantaneous. Trust takes time to earn.

Let's say a pedophile repents and becomes a Christian. The church should forgive him because God says that old things are passed away and all things become new. But the church would be foolish to allow him to be a counselor in junior camp the next summer. He could say, "You haven't really forgiven me." But every parent would say, "There's a difference between forgiveness and trust." Trust takes a long time to restore.

Let's say your daughter is engaged to marry a young man in six weeks when she discovers that he's become addicted to cocaine and owes twenty thousand dollars to his dealers. Her fiancé begs for forgiveness. As a Christian, she should forgive him. But she shouldn't marry him. He could protest, "You haven't really forgiven me!" By releasing her bitterness, refusing to hurt him in return, and treating him with kindness, she has forgiven him. But marriage must be built on trust, and she would be foolish to enter the marriage without allowing time for trust to be rebuilt.

Be careful that you don't take this qualifier to an extreme. If you've been wounded, it's tempting to use your pain as an opportunity to gain control—to use the offense as leverage for years to come. "Trust hasn't yet been restored," you might claim and continue to rub your offender's nose in his mistake every chance you get, to keep him humble and controllable. That's not forgiveness. If repentance and change have taken place, trust must eventually be restored.

THE STEPS TO FORGIVENESS

The *Los Angeles Times* recently reported that the Templeton Foundation gave a $10 million grant to a team of psychologists, sociologists, and neuroscientists, earmarked for "forgiveness research." The researchers determined that the problem with forgiveness is that most people are willing to forgive but don't know how. They concluded that the ingredients required for forgiving someone included facing up to the fact that you've been hurt, giving up the grudge, and choosing to show mercy. They spent $10 million to confirm that the Bible's teachings are true. God commanded, "Do not take revenge.... Do not be overcome by evil, but overcome evil with good" (Romans 12:19, 21).

Here are some practical guidelines for developing a forgiving spirit:

Choose to Forgive

You are commanded to forgive. Jesus would not command you to do something you cannot do. Forgiveness isn't something you feel like doing; it usually runs counter to your instincts. Forgiveness is an act of the will, a mental decision. You choose to forgive regardless of your feelings because it's the right thing to do.

Pray

I have a lot of faults, but I can honestly say that I don't hold a grudge against anyone. I've been seriously hurt before, and there are a few people who refuse to speak to me. But I don't harbor resentment. That's a liberating feeling.

chapter 3

Part of the reason I've been able to remain free from bitterness is that when I pray each morning, "Help me to forgive my debtors today," I give God the names of the people with whom I'm angry. I pray, "Lord, help me not to hold a grudge against that letter writer who said all I cared about was money, or the preacher who accused me of compromising and said I was going to burn in hell, or the writer who suggested I was building a monument to myself." I remember those things, and they hurt; but I pray, "Help me not to retaliate, Lord. Help me to remember how much you have forgiven me."

Dr. David Jeremiah, in his book *Prayer: The Great Adventure*, suggests that most of our everyday grievances can be dealt with through intercession and not personal involvement. "In your prayer each day," Jeremiah writes, "you can build the foundation of a forgiving spirit to sustain you even before you have been injured."[9] You will encounter wrongdoers each day. Someone will cut you off on the highway, or shortchange you, or speak behind your back—or it may be much more serious. Pray each day that God will give you a spirit of forgiveness toward those who become indebted to you.

When someone has committed a more serious act against you, pray that God will give you the strength and wisdom to confront him or her if necessary and to forgive at the proper time. And pray that God will bless the one who wronged you.

Give Yourself Some Time

The Bible says, "They that wait upon the LORD shall renew their strength" (Isaiah 40:31 KJV). When you've been hurt, don't make a quick, emotional decision about how to respond. Some people react in anger and later regret what they've done. Others know they're not supposed to hold a grudge, but they "forgive" too easily and too quickly. Les and Leslie Parrott spoke of "trigger-happy forgivers" who try to avoid pain. They think, "I'll put up with this horrible treatment because I don't know what I'll have without it."[10] That kind of behavior doesn't motivate repentance in the perpetrator and merely puts a mask over the real pain.

If you're enabling immoral behavior to continue, that's not forgiveness. At the moment of the offense, don't be too quick to retaliate or to forgive. Tell the perpetrator, "I need some time to pray about this and react properly." Then temporarily put some distance between the two of you so you can pray and seek counsel. When the offense is serious, I suggest you read one or all of the following books: *Love Must Be Tough* by James Dobson,[11] *Door of Hope* (written especially for physical or sexual abuse victims) by Jan Frank,[12] and *Boundaries* by Henry Cloud and John Townsend.[13]

Seek Wise Christian Counsel

Don't dump your problems on just anyone who will listen. Don't recruit people against the one who has offended you. Don't try to get people to feel sorry for you.

But seek wisdom. When someone wounds you and you're having difficulty forgiving, confess to a trusted Christian friend your temptation to be embittered, and ask for help in praying that you'll be able to forgive. The Bible says, "As iron sharpens iron, so one man sharpens another" (Proverbs 27:17). If the offense is serious, be humble enough to go to a trained Christian counselor and ask for guidance.

Lovingly Confront the Issue If Necessary

Sometimes you need to forgive the offense, drop the matter, and go on with your life. But if the offense is serious, if it is ongoing, or if it is causing bitterness to be stored up in you, you may need to lovingly and tactfully confront the one who has wronged you. Paul wrote, "Brothers, if someone is caught in a sin, you who are spiritual should restore him gently" (Galatians 6:1).

A victim, especially when the perpetrator is a close relative, is often tempted to feel guilty or take blame for things that were not his or her fault. At times, it is important that you place the blame squarely where it belongs, which may require a confrontation. (The three books I mentioned earlier would be extremely helpful in this step as well.) Confrontation should not occur without some guidance from a trusted Christian counselor or minister. But in serious matters, it is an important and necessary step toward genuine forgiveness.

Express Kindness to the One Who Offended You

The Scripture commands, "If your enemy is hungry, feed him; if he is thirsty, give him something to drink" (Romans 12:20). This is where genuine forgiveness takes place. When you express kindness to your offender, you have released your right to retaliate. Sometimes the relationship may be changed forever. A scar may remain. Trust may not be restored. Your offender may reject your kind gestures. But you have released your bitterness, and the process of healing has begun.

FORGIVENESS SETS YOU FREE

When we display a forgiving spirit, the results are freedom and victory. Satan wants to deceive you into thinking that if you forgive, you lose and the offender wins. But just the opposite is true. If you harbor hatred, you lose. Resentment doesn't hurt the person you hate nearly as much as it damages you. Someone said, "Bitterness is the poison you swallow hoping the other guy dies."

How did you react when you read the illustration I used at the beginning of the chapter? You may have thought, *Bob, you're not suggesting that Jane should just forgive and give Ralph her blessing in this new marriage, are you?*

Well, yes and no. She shouldn't endorse a relationship that clearly is outside of God's will. But she should forgive. Forgiveness is for her sake, not his. Forgiveness is not saying what he did was right. Forgiveness is saying,

"I release my right to retaliate. I was wronged, but I will not spend the rest of my life trying to get even with you." Forgiveness frees God to do his work of justice and frees Jane from the bonds of bitterness. Jane wins.

That's why Jesus commanded you to forgive. He said:

> I tell you who hear me: Love your enemies, do good to those who hate you, bless those who curse you, pray for those who mistreat you. If someone strikes you on one cheek, turn to him the other also. If someone takes your cloak, do not stop him from taking your tunic. (Luke 6:27–29)

Jesus didn't leave you an option. It's a command because he wants what's best for you. If you harbor hatred very long, it eats away at your personality, your health, your concentration, and your relationships—and it destroys you. When you're big enough to forgive, you pour out the resentment, and you win.

John D. Beckett, in his book *Loving Monday*, wrote:

> I had just turned thirteen, and I was enjoying a short but very special vacation with my dad at my uncle's summer cottage in Canada's north woods, six hundred miles from home. There, trouble found us when...Uncle Harold got the notion that his young nephew might like to look over his favorite playing cards which featured—you guessed it—a gallery of

well-endowed naked women. As I was gawking at pose after enticing pose, Dad walked into the room.... Quickly taking in the situation, Dad exploded. Here was his own brother, nearly sixty—not some misguided youngster—callously exposing his son, John, to a tawdry and shameful display. "Pack your bags, John," Dad fumed. "We're going home."

A few minutes later we crawled into our small cedar boat. With a single pull, Dad started the outboard motor and we pulled away from the dock. I bit into my lip, attempting to mask my intense disappointment. Why did this very special outing with Dad have to abort in a rage of tempers and harsh words?

A hundred yards from the shore...Dad said grimly, "John, we're going back." I was sure he'd forgotten something important.

In the distance, I could see Uncle Harold standing at the cottage window, staring out at the lake. As the boat drew nearer, he began trudging down to the dock to find out what had gone wrong. Then I saw something else. In those brief moments, Dad's intense, righteous anger had met with an equally powerful and deep love for his brother. The former was giving way to the latter. Dad was coming back to make things right. Too many years. Too many shared experiences. Too much was at stake to allow this incident to become a festering wound, one that might never heal.

chapter 3

My head still swirling, I watched in amazement as these two forceful, strong-willed brothers met on the dock and reached out at the same moment into a prolonged embrace. Few words were spoken. Few were needed. They understood. Never again would Harold violate Reg's fatherly care for his son. Never again would he underestimate Dad's intense sense of right and wrong or risk such a breach.

...Dad's passion for his beliefs had caused him to risk fracture with the eldest of his five brothers. Yet, without compromising that passion, he had found a place for forgiveness and reconciliation.[14]

Do you need to find that place of forgiveness and reconciliation? It begins on your knees, when you pray, "Father, forgive me my debts as I forgive...." I hope it will end for you as it did for John Beckett's dad—with a compassionate embrace and a restored relationship. But even if restoration is impossible, be faithful. Let Jesus transform your bitterness into forgiveness and set you free.

PRAYER Starter:

> *Dear Heavenly Father, you are perfect and I, like Paul, am the chief of sinners. How can I measure what you have done for me? You have forgiven so much. I know that for me to harbor bitterness in my heart is to continue in my sinful state. I know that bitterness harms*

me more than it does the person I hate. Lord, I need
somehow to release the bitterness I feel against
_____. What he/she did was wrong,
Lord—terribly wrong. But I know that the debt he/she
owes me is no greater than the debt I owed to you,
which you willingly forgave. Today I am choosing to
forgive _____. Please grant me strength and
wisdom that I might find a way to express kindness.
Help me not to have unrealistic expectations about
his/her response. I am choosing forgiveness. I know that
trust may take a lifetime to restore. But I can choose
today to forgive. Thank you for forgiving me, and for
giving me the power to release my bitterness.

DISCUSSION Questions

1. List some of the most serious sins from your past that God has forgiven. (You might want to write in code in case someone finds this book!) What sins in your life did God forgive yesterday? Today? When you consider the four categories of sin mentioned in this chapter, how many sins do you think you commit in one day?

2. What is harder for you—to receive God's forgiveness or to extend it to others? Why is forgiveness so difficult?

3. What is the meaning of "Forgive and you will be forgiven"? Why is forgiveness important for Christians?

4. Whom do you need to forgive? Identify the person(s) by name. What will happen to that person if you choose forgiveness over bitterness? What will happen to you?

I am now the most

miserable man living.

To remain as I am

is impossible.

I must die or be better.

—Abraham Lincoln

I have told you this so that my
joy may be in you and that
your joy may be complete.

—Jesus Christ

FROM depression TO joy

We're writing this chapter the week of September 11, 2001. Americans have been glued to television sets all week long, hoping to find some encouraging news after terrorists hijacked three commercial jets and crashed them into the two World Trade Center towers and the Pentagon. A fourth hijacking failed to reach its destination, apparently because passengers overpowered the hijackers and crashed the plane in a field near Pittsburgh, Pennsylvania. At this time we don't know the death toll, but it will be in the thousands. America is shocked, angry, and depressed.

The Bible warns, "There will be terrible times in the

last days. People will be lovers of themselves, lovers of money, boastful, proud, abusive, disobedient to their parents, ungrateful, unholy, without love, unforgiving, slanderous, without self-control, brutal, not lovers of the good" (2 Timothy 3:1–3). We are living in terrible times—sin is rampant. When Satan overcomes people, they "invent ways of doing evil" (Romans 1:30). Watching those scriptures be fulfilled before our very eyes can be downright depressing.

But it's not just the news that can be depressing. So many things go wrong in our personal lives and bring us down. Children rebel, loved ones die, jobs are lost, friends disappoint us, our health fails…. In a world tainted by sin, it can be difficult to stay positive.

Jesus gave this invitation to all who are disenchanted with life: "Come to me, all you who are weary and burdened, and I will give you rest. Take my yoke upon you and learn from me, for I am gentle and humble in heart, and you will find rest for your souls" (Matthew 11:28–29). The Christian personality should be characterized by joy and peace, not depression and turmoil. That's not an easy transformation to make, but with Christ's help, you can do it!

A BIBLICAL EXAMPLE OF DEPRESSION

The prophet Elijah was depressed. The Scripture tells us, "He came to a broom tree, sat down under it and prayed that he might die. 'I have had enough, LORD,' he said. 'Take my life; I am no better than my ancestors'" (1 Kings 19:4).

Why was Elijah so despondent? It seemed totally out of character for a man of God. I can think of several reasons why he should *not* have become depressed:

(1) He was *a godly prophet* who stood boldly before the wicked king Ahab and warned that God would judge the nation's sin with a prolonged drought. When the famine did come as he predicted, Elijah was forced to flee for his life; but while he was in hiding, God sustained him by feeding him miraculously every day.

(2) Elijah was also *a powerful miracle-worker*. While a fugitive in a foreign land, he lived with a widow and her son. Upon Elijah's promise, their food supply was never depleted—their last jar of flour never ran out, and the last jug of oil never ran dry. When the widow's son mysteriously and suddenly died, Elijah raised him from the dead!

(3) He was also *a courageous leader.* After three and one-half years of drought, Elijah came out of hiding and challenged 450 prophets of Baal to a contest to determine the one true God: "Let's build two altars, one to your god Baal and one to my God Jehovah, and let's see which is capable of sending fire down from heaven to burn the sacrifice." His enemies agreed, and the contest began. The prophets of Baal pleaded with their god for an entire day to bring down fire from heaven. They finally gave up. Then Elijah prayed a simple prayer to Jehovah, and fire came down from heaven to consume the sacrifice and everything around it. The crowd of

onlookers fell to their knees and cried out, "Yahweh is God! Yahweh is God!"

With so much in Elijah's favor, why did he become depressed? How quickly things can change! With the new wave of public opinion in his favor, Elijah ordered the execution of all the false prophets so the malignancy of idol worship could be excised permanently from Israel. Then Elijah announced to the king, "Since the people have repented, God will send rain for your crops." That same day a soaking, refreshing, desperately needed rain came, just as Elijah had predicted. The Bible says that the Spirit of the Lord then came upon Elijah, and he ran all the way to Jezreel—a distance of about eighteen miles. He was so jubilant, he beat the chariot the king was riding in! But the wicked queen Jezebel was not happy about the changing of the guard and the execution of her favorite prophets. She sent this message to Elijah: "May the gods deal with me, be it ever so severely, if by this time tomorrow I do not make your life like that of one of them" (1 Kings 19:2).

Elijah was suddenly and uncharacteristically afraid. He fled for his life.

After an exhausting day's journey into the desert, Elijah sat under a broom tree and prayed that he might die. Just one day after a high point in his life, this godly, miracle-working, courageous, energetic prophet was giving up and longing for death.

FOUR CAUSES OF DEPRESSION

Maybe you can identify with Elijah's depression.

More than seventeen million Americans suffer from depression. The resulting absenteeism and loss of productivity is estimated to cost American businesses (and ultimately each of us as consumers) more than $20 billion annually.[1] Edward F. Ziegler calls depression "the common cold of psychological disorders."

Les Carter, in his book *Mind Over Emotions*, gives this clinical definition of depression: "A feeling of sadness and dejection, accompanied by a gloomy mindset.... It can last anywhere from a few hours to several months, or in rare cases even years. Depression is distinguished from simple unhappiness by being more prolonged than the circumstances responsible for it warrant."[2] According to Carter, common symptoms of depression include insomnia, changes in appetite, and loss of pleasure in activities that once were enjoyable. Depressed people often have difficulty concentrating, develop pessimistic thinking patterns, and withdraw from others.[3]

Four degrees or stages of depression have been identified: *dejection*—a temporary emotional valley; *discouragement*—a temporary feeling of hopelessness and loss of enthusiasm; *despondency*—intense melancholy feelings that can last for weeks or months, accompanied by dramatic changes in eating habits and sleeping patterns; and *despair*—a dangerous stage of emotional instability where pessimistic feelings, irrationality, and thoughts of death overwhelm a person.

Christians who don't get depressed are tempted to dismiss all melancholy moods as being out of sync with God's will. They might flippantly advise the depressed person to "snap out of it," "get a grip," or "get happy." But the problem often is too complex to be overcome by a simple motivational speech. Depression has many causes, but most fall into the following four categories:

Temperamental

I think Elijah was prone to bouts with depression because of his innate temperament. Each person is "wired" differently. Some are born with easygoing, phlegmatic temperaments, and they hardly ever get depressed. Their steadiness has little to do with faith or spiritual depth—they're just born that way. Others with more sanguine temperaments, like Simon Peter, are up and down like yo-yos. They're jubilant one day and in the pits the next. But they don't stay down very long. Some people, like Doubting Thomas, have melancholy personalities. They're perfectionistic and pragmatic. They see the potential problems more than the bright side—the glass is always half empty instead of half full. These people can get depressed for weeks at a time.

In addition to Elijah, many other great leaders throughout history had personalities that were prone to depression: Moses, Paul, Martin Luther, Charles Spurgeon, Winston Churchill, and Abraham Lincoln all experienced dark periods in their lives, and several of them even contemplated suicide.

The good news is that the Spirit of Christ living in you can help you overcome the dark side of your temperament. It's not God's will for you to make yourself and others close to you miserable because of your ugly moods. As you begin allowing Jesus Christ to be the Lord of your personality, the down times will become less severe and less frequent. You may always battle against the darkness of depression, much like a person prone to obesity must work harder to stay healthy. But if you put into practice the suggestions at the end of this chapter and allow God to begin the transformation, your battle will get easier with time.

Circumstantial

Some circumstances understandably lead to temporary periods of depression.

A preacher I know was approached by a young couple in his church. "Will you please talk to my father?" the young wife asked. "He's been so down for several weeks, and we can't get him to cheer up."

"Has anything happened in his life that would take him down?" the preacher asked.

"Well, my mom died," the woman answered. "But that was several months ago. He should be over it by now!"

The depression that results from losing someone close to you is a natural and, for most, inevitable part of life. Bereavement can take months and sometimes years to work through. That's why when the patriarchs died in the Old Testament, God appointed a prolonged period of mourning so the people would have opportunity to grieve the one who was lost and to work through the natural cycle of depression that follows a loved one's death.

Any dramatic event can trigger depression, especially if the event is one of the major "Ds"—*death, disease, divorce,* or *disaster.* Paul wrestled with depression when he suffered severe hardships. He wrote:

> We do not want you to be uninformed, brothers, about the hardships we suffered in the province of Asia. We were under great pressure, far beyond our ability to endure, so that we despaired even of life. Indeed, in our hearts we felt the sentence of death. But this happened that we might not rely on ourselves but on God, who raises the dead. (2 Corinthians 1:8–9)

Three circumstances in Elijah's life probably provoked his depression:

A Great Victory

Elijah had just won a major victory on Mt. Carmel. He literally had a mountaintop experience with God. Everyone wants to win and be on the mountain peak, but one of the bad things about mountaintop experiences is that the only direction you can go afterward is down. The aftermath of a great victory is a prime time for depression.

I remember the day we brought our first child home from the hospital. We were on a high. The grandparents were there, and people from the church visited, and everybody made a big deal about the new baby. That afternoon I went up to the bedroom to check on my wife and found her lying on the bed, weeping. She seldom cries. "What's wrong?" I asked, but she couldn't explain— she just felt down in the dumps. We had a healthy baby, and my wife was in good health—we had much to be thankful for. I couldn't understand her feelings. I didn't know anything about postpartum depression. At about 2:00 A.M. when the baby was still crying and I couldn't sleep, I began to understand her depression!

Every victory has a downside, and every high has a commensurate low. Have you ever watched your favorite ball team win a crucial game over the archrival, only to let down in the next game and lose to a much less formidable foe? Or maybe you get the blues in January, after the Christmas holidays are over. I do!

Every Monday morning many preachers battle what Archibald Hart, professor of psychology at Fuller Theological Seminary, termed "post-adrenaline depression." On Sunday victories were won (or at least the sermon got done in time), and the resulting adrenaline rush puts the minister on a high. On Monday he comes crashing down.

Legend has it that Alexander the Great wept after he had conquered the world, saying, "There are no more worlds to conquer."

Highly motivated people are especially vulnerable to depression. We expect the exultation of success to continue, but it doesn't. Sometimes we get disgusted with ourselves and think, *I should be on top of the world. I've got so much to be thankful for, yet I'm depressed. What's wrong with me?*

A Significant Failure

Not only had Elijah just come off a mountaintop experience with God, he also came into the valley to meet Jezebel. Even with the assistance of fire from heaven, Elijah couldn't win favor with the wicked queen. When she heard that Elijah had executed all her favorite prophets, she was incensed: "So Jezebel sent a messenger to Elijah to say, 'May the gods deal with me, be it ever so severely, if by this time tomorrow I do not make your life like that of one of them'" (1 Kings 19:2).

Elijah had a contract on his life. That would depress most people! The prophet had won a great victory only to discover the queen was still out to get him. Instead of repenting, she was more resolved than ever to spread wickedness. Elijah's problems had only increased.

Loneliness

Elijah ran, alone, into the desert. There he told God that Jezebel had killed all God's prophets and that he was the only one left. He was exaggerating his problem, which depression will cause you to do. Nevertheless, he felt alone. If you feel that you've been left alone and that no one cares about you, you are a prime candidate for depression. The college student away from home for the first time, the newly widowed, the soldier just shipped overseas, and the single mom often battle depression more than others.

Do you know what five-year age span has the highest suicide rate? The National Center for Health Statistics reports that the age group with the highest suicide rate is not the much publicized teen group, but eighty- to eighty-four-year-olds, with the highest rate among those who are divorced or widowed.[4] That ought to be a wake-up call to churches. There is a tremendous need for ministry to the elderly because so many of them are lonely.

The psalmist wrote, "I am like a desert owl, like an owl among the ruins. I lie awake; I have become like a bird alone on a roof" (Psalm 102:6–7). When you're depressed, you're tempted to withdraw from people. You don't want to fake it and pretend everything is fine when it isn't. Being around happy people underscores your misery, and you're turned off by bubbly personalities. So you stay at home or sulk in a corner, feeling more and more unloved and unwanted. It's a cycle—the more you withdraw, the more you feel unloved, and the more you want to withdraw.

Dr. Philip Zimbardo, professor of psychology at Stanford University, wrote, "I know of no more potent killer than isolation. There is no more destructive influence on physical and mental health than the isolation of you from me and us from them."[5]

During World War II the Nazis discovered that the most effective type of torture for forcing prisoners of war to give up secrets was nothing more than solitary confinement. After just a few days of total isolation, most men would tell all.

God knows we need each other to fight effectively against the enemy. That's why his Word says, "Encourage one another daily, as long as it is called Today, so that none of you may be hardened by sin's deceitfulness" (Hebrews 3:13).

Psychological

A third reason for depression has to do with our own thought patterns.

Psychologists say that the number one cause of depression is *repressed anger*. People are angry at others, themselves, or even God. They internalize their anger, begin feeling sorry for themselves, and become depressed.

Elijah had reason to be angry. But he reacted to Jezebel's threat not with anger at Jezebel or with faith in

God, but with *fear*. "Elijah was *afraid* and ran for his life" (1 Kings 19:3).

How could a man stand up against 450 false prophets, then run like a coward because of the threat of one woman? For one thing, Jezebel was a vicious, powerful, intimidating woman. But another reason is simply that Elijah's mental outlook wasn't right. He had lost sight of God. When we start to get depressed, our thinking can become distorted. I heard Zig Ziglar refer to this as "stinkin' thinkin'." Elijah should have remembered that God would protect him. But when negative thinking began to dominate his thoughts, he fell into self-pity, forgot God's power, and ran for his life.

Elijah must have thought, *Nothing has changed. Jezebel is still running the country. My victory was hollow. All my efforts are futile.* Think of the things you've heard people say that reveal their feelings of futility:

"I try to be a loving mate. I make all kinds of sacrifices, and she doesn't even notice. What's the use?"

"I try to be a good parent, but it makes no difference. I rush home from work, fix a decent meal, try to be nice to everyone—and all they do is gripe. Nothing I do matters."

"We try to get out of debt, but we just can't seem to make it. We discipline ourselves, stick to a budget, we do without the things we want...and then the car breaks down and we spend a thousand dollars repairing it. It's futile!"

"This year I told myself I was going to be the best schoolteacher ever. I decided I was really going to make a difference in the classroom. But the kids are out of control, and if I discipline them, the parents complain. The administrator criticizes everything I do. I keep thinking, *Why bother?*"

Dr. David Burns, in his book *Feeling Good: The New Mood Therapy*, gives us hope. "Most depression arises from erroneous thinking," Burns writes. "We have it within our power to control…the thoughts that dupe us into needless gloom."[6] Whether your depression is caused by futile thinking, repressed anger, or fear, there is good news: You don't have to continue on with your "stinkin' thinkin'."

Physical

Medical researchers have discovered that some people have a chemical imbalance of serotonin—a chemical in the brain—that makes them more prone to prolonged feelings of despondency. That's why medicines that modulate neurotransmitter levels help some people with bipolar or manic-depressive disorders.

Drugs should not be the first recourse. I've seen mind-altering drugs prescribed too quickly to people who have a sin problem, not a physical disorder. But I also have seen those with serious disorders helped by medication. If a respected doctor diagnoses you or someone you love with a chemical imbalance that is causing depression, get a second opinion. After you've consulted two or more physicians, if it's clear that you have a physical problem, be grateful that we live in a time when God has enabled researchers to discover medicines to treat the problem.

Chemical imbalances also can be self-induced. People who take illegal drugs or drink alcohol can find themselves battling cycles of depression that are caused by the very substances they hoped would help. A depressed person might take drugs or drink alcohol to try to escape his or her problems. But when the effects of the drugs wear off, the problems are compounded, and the temptation to take more drugs is intensified. An addiction has formed, and the person is in a cycle he or she cannot break out of alone.

Even things like a poor diet, lack of exercise, or physical exhaustion can affect serotonin levels and exacerbate feelings of depression. It's no secret that the more tired you feel, the more likely you are to feel depressed. Elijah was exhausted not only from extreme mental anguish (he had been on an emotional roller coaster) but also from extreme physical stress. When the rain first fell, he had run eighteen miles to reach the capital city, Jezreel, as quickly as he could. Then, when Jezebel threatened to take his life, he turned around and ran again. For most of the next day, he traveled deep into the desert. At the point of total exhaustion, Elijah sat down under a broom tree and prayed that God would take his life.

God's servants are not exempt from the consequences of fatigue. No matter how healthy, energetic, or motivated you think you are, you have limited physical resources. If you burn the candle at both ends, eventually it will burn out. When you're exhausted, you're vulnerable to depression.

When a woman in the crowd touched the hem of Jesus' garment and was healed, Jesus stopped and asked, "Who touched me?" The disciples reminded him that many people were bumping into him in the crowd, but Jesus responded, "No—someone touched me. I felt the power go out from me" (Luke 8:45–46, paraphrased). If you're in the business of dealing with the public—healing, counseling, teaching, guiding, or assisting—then you know the emotional exhaustion that can result from your job. Your efforts deplete your energy. Your work drains you of power. Be aware of your human limitations. The more fatigued you are, the more susceptible you'll be to depression.

DO YOU WANT TO GET WELL?

When Jesus met a man by the pool of Bethesda who had been disabled for thirty-eight years, he asked the man what seems, at first glance, to be a strange question: "Do you want to get well?" (John 5:6). But it's not really a strange question at all. Some sick people don't want to get well. They like feeling sorry for themselves. They like not having to be responsible. They like lying by the pool with nothing to do.

Some people make a career out of ugly moods. It's the way they manipulate and control people. It may be the only way they get attention. Make a decision today that you don't want to be like that. Decide that you want to get better.

Drs. Minirth and Meier contend strongly that "the emotional pain of clinical depression is a totally unnecessary, totally avoidable experience."[7] I love the title of their book—*Happiness Is a Choice*. Without Jesus Christ, that may not be true. But "I can do everything through him who gives me strength" (Philippians 4:13); I can even change my depression to joy.

Paul wrote the Book of Philippians from a prison cell, yet the book is full of references to his joy and contentment. In that letter we are commanded, "Rejoice in the Lord always. I will say it again: Rejoice!" (Philippians 4:4).

Happiness is not the result of perfect circumstances, perfect relationships, or perfect health—it's the result of a good attitude in spite of problems. If you will be happy only when everything in life is ideal, you have a long wait ahead of you! Life will never be perfect. Jesus said, "I have told you these things, so that in me you may have peace. In this world you will have trouble. But take heart! I have overcome the world" (John 16:33).

Francie Baltazar-Schwartz, in the book *Chicken Soup for the Soul at Work*, tells about a guy named Jerry who was always in a good mood and always had something positive to say. If you asked, "How are you, Jerry?" he'd say, "If I were any better, I'd be twins!"

Schwartz wrote:

One day I said [to Jerry], "I don't get it. You can't possibly be a positive, up person all the time. How do you do it?"

chapter 4

Jerry replied, "Each morning I wake up and say to myself, 'Jerry, you have two choices today. You can choose to be in a good mood or you can choose to be in a bad mood.' I choose to be in a good mood."

"It's not that easy," I protested.

"Yes it is," Jerry said. "Life is all about choices. When you cut out all the junk, every situation is a choice."

Several years ago the restaurant Jerry owns was robbed. The thieves panicked and shot him. Jerry recalled that day:

When I was lying on the floor, I remembered I had two choices. I could choose to live or I could choose to die. I chose to live. The paramedics were great. They kept saying I was going to be fine. But when they wheeled me into the emergency room and I saw the expressions on the faces of the doctors and nurses, I got really scared. In their eyes I read, "He's a dead man." I knew I needed to take action.

There was a big burly nurse shouting questions at me. She asked, "Are you allergic to anything?"

"Yes," I replied. The doctors and nurses stopped working as they waited for my reply. "Bullets!" Over their laughter I told them, "I am choosing to live. Operate on me as if I am alive, not dead."

After eighteen hours of surgery and weeks of intensive care, Jerry lived, thanks to the skill of his doctors, but thanks also to his amazing attitude and to God's grace.

Schwartz said, "I saw Jerry six months after the accident and asked, 'How are you doing?' He said, 'If I were any better, I'd be twins.'"[8]

Decide today that you want to get well—that no matter your circumstances, you are willing to let Christ transform you from depression to joy.

GOD'S PRESCRIPTION FOR CURING DEPRESSION

The Bible promises that God "comforts the downcast" (2 Corinthians 7:6). When Elijah despaired even of life, God appeared to him. God did four things for Elijah that cured his depression—four things that provide a perfect prescription for overcoming nearly every kind of depression. I don't want to pretend that a person who has a chemical imbalance or a serious psychological disorder can suddenly get well the way Elijah did. But most of us can moderate our personalities with God's help if we'll follow this prescription and allow Jesus Christ to transform us from depression to joy.

Recuperation

God first took care of Elijah's physical needs.

Then [Elijah] lay down under the tree and fell asleep. All at once an angel touched him and said, "Get up and eat." He looked around, and there by his head was a cake of bread baked over hot coals, and a jar of water. He ate and drank and then lay down again. (1 Kings 19:5–6)

chapter 4

God was kind to Elijah. He didn't chastise him for having a sour attitude or lecture him about faith and courage. God just let him rest and provided something for him to eat so his body could recover.

Know When to Stop Working

Perhaps you were raised with a strong work ethic and feel most fulfilled when you're working hard and accomplishing something. That's good! The Bible says, "Lazy hands make a man poor, but diligent hands bring wealth" (Proverbs 10:4) and "Whatever you do, work at it with all your heart, as working for the Lord, not for men" (Colossians 3:23). But some people take that good work ethic to the extreme and drive themselves to the point of exhaustion because they don't know how to rest.

Are you one of those people who has a hard time resting? Do you take work home with you? Do you use your in-home fax machine to keep work flowing and keep your cell phone on all hours of the day and night? When you go on a vacation, do you make your family miserable because you refuse to make a pit stop on a three-hour trip? Do you try to cram as much into your vacation day as possible to keep from getting bored, then call back to the office every hour because you're fretting over the work you're missing? Are your vacations more exhausting than your work?

One of the most spiritual things you can do is learn to rest and recuperate. Learn to relax. The Jews were commanded to rest one day out of every seven. They also celebrated several holidays throughout the year in which they were to do no work. Then, every seventh year, the whole nation took a sabbatical! God wanted them to learn how to rest, to experience the change of pace, and to refresh themselves.

Jesus' ministry lasted only three and one-half years, yet he spent the first six weeks on a personal retreat in the wilderness! Throughout his ministry he occasionally went into the mountains to pray alone. He would sometimes say to his disciples, "Let's go to the other side of the lake, away from the crowds." With all the stress that was around him, he could still lie down in a boat and go to sleep in the midst of a storm. Jesus knew how to rest. He had balance in his life.

I don't do a lot of things well, but I think I've learned how to shift gears and relax on occasion. It's not uncommon for me to work fourteen or fifteen hours a day for two or three weeks in a row—it's just the nature of my occupation. But then I take two or three days off to rest and relax—on a golf trip with some friends or an overnight trip with my wife. In the summer I take five weeks away from work. I read that if a preacher is good, he deserves at least four weeks of vacation; if he isn't good, the congregation deserves it!

A couple of summers ago, I did something I had never done: I got out my laptop computer and learned to play Hearts. It would be wrong for me to sit in the office and play Hearts. But it also would be wrong for me to spend my whole vacation writing sermons on that laptop. So I spent time doing something purposeless. I got pretty good at the game! Somehow beating three fictitious people on the computer was very gratifying!

God commanded, "Be still, and know that I am God" (Psalm 46:10). Somebody said, "If you can't at times do something totally purposeless, perhaps it's because you don't believe in the sovereignty of God." Learn to slow down, shift gears, relax, and refresh yourself. It's amazing how just a little rest can renew our spirits and replenish our internal resources.

Eat Right and Exercise

God also made sure Elijah was eating properly. An unhealthy diet and lack of exercise will exacerbate depression. Eat right, exercise regularly, and give yourself the proper amounts of sleep, and you'll have a much easier time keeping the blues at bay. God knew what Elijah needed, so he sent an angel to minister to his physical needs. The angel commanded him, "Get up and eat," and then let him go back to sleep. If God sent an angel to minister to your physical needs, what would the angel tell you to do? He might tell you to put the potato chips away, turn off the television, and take a walk with a friend. It's difficult to overcome depression without eating right, exercising regularly, and sleeping well.

Revelation

God helped Elijah get his mind off himself and onto the awesome power of God. After he had been rejuvenated, Elijah received a revelation from the Lord. God said, "Go out and stand on the mountain in the presence of the LORD, for the LORD is about to pass by" (1 Kings 19:11).

Then Elijah saw three impressive evidences of God's power, followed by the presence of God himself.

> Then a great and powerful wind tore the mountains apart and shattered the rocks before the LORD, but the LORD was not in the wind. After the wind there was an earthquake, but the LORD was not in the earthquake. After the earthquake came a fire, but the LORD was not in the fire. And after the fire came a gentle whisper. When Elijah heard it, he pulled his cloak over his face and went out and stood at the mouth of the cave. Then a voice said to him, "What are you doing here, Elijah?" (1 Kings 19:11–13)

Elijah got depressed because he had taken his eyes off God and had begun focusing on himself. Before God arrived, Elijah was having a real pity party. He felt unappreciated, unproductive, and unloved. But once he got his eyes off of himself and saw the tornado, the earthquake, and the fire, he realized that God was so much more powerful than all his problems. He was ready to listen to the still, small voice of God again.

We erroneously think that the way out of our depression is to analyze ourselves, understand our past, and focus on getting our needs met. But what we usually need is to forget about ourselves and focus our thoughts on God. "Why are you downcast, O my soul? Why so disturbed within me? Put your hope in God, for I will yet praise him, my Savior and my God" (Psalm 42:5–6). How can you allow Jesus to transform you from depression to joy unless you're willing to focus on him and listen for his revelation? Jesus will reveal himself to you primarily through his Word and through his Church. It sounds like a simple answer, but it's good advice: When you're depressed, go back to the basics of Bible reading and corporate worship.

Read Your Bible

When you are depressed, read your Bible and allow God to nourish your soul. The wife of one of our staff members has battled depression for years. She hasn't always won; sometimes depression has gotten the best of her. She's taken medication without much relief. But she told me there are certain scriptures that have sustained her throughout her struggle:

- In the same way, the Spirit helps us in our weakness. We do not know what we ought to pray for, but the Spirit himself intercedes for us with groans that words cannot express. (Romans 8:26)

- Who is he that condemns? Christ Jesus, who died—more than that, who was raised to life—is at the right hand of God and is also interceding for us. (Romans 8:34)
- But he said to me, "My grace is sufficient for you, for my power is made perfect in weakness." Therefore I will boast all the more gladly about my weaknesses, so that Christ's power may rest on me. (2 Corinthians 12:9)
- "My soul is overwhelmed with sorrow to the point of death," [Jesus] said to them. "Stay here and keep watch." Going a little farther, he fell to the ground and prayed that if possible the hour might pass from him. (Mark 14:34–35)

Jesus revealed himself to her through those scriptures. She realized that Jesus really did know what she was going through and that he was interceding for her.

Go to Church

Force yourself to go to worship with God's people. The Bible commands you to "Make a joyful noise unto the LORD" (Psalm 100:1 KJV) and to "sing and make music in your heart to the Lord" (Ephesians 5:19). When you're down, the worst thing you can do is stay home from church.

A philosopher once said, "If you act the way you wish you felt, you'll eventually feel the way you're acting." Don't wait until you feel like going to church. Get up, go to worship, and sing the songs even though you don't feel like it. Allow God to reveal himself to you and to replenish your thirsty soul.

Responsibility

God came to Elijah in a still, small voice and asked, "What are you doing here, Elijah?" (1 Kings 19:13). "He replied, 'I have been very zealous for the LORD God Almighty. The Israelites have rejected your covenant, broken down your altars, and put your prophets to death with the sword. I am the only one left, and now they are trying to kill me too'" (1 Kings 19:14).

Notice how God helped Elijah overcome his depression by giving him a new challenge: "The LORD said to him, 'Go back the way you came, and go to the Desert of Damascus. When you get there, anoint Hazael king over Aram. Also, anoint Jehu son of Nimshi king over Israel, and anoint Elisha son of Shaphat from Abel Meholah to succeed you as prophet'" (1 Kings 19:15–16).

God didn't promise Elijah exemption from Jezebel's wrath; he just gave Elijah a new responsibility. "I want you to go right back to work and anoint some new kings," God was saying to Elijah. "I want you to open a school for training new prophets who can take your place, and get ready to hand over the reigns to Elisha. I'm going to expand your ministry."

When you get depressed, you don't usually need pity as much as you need a new challenge—a new goal in life. When we're depressed, we develop bad habits. We lie on the couch, watch too much television, overeat, and throw pity parties. We get into cycles that are hard to break. You have to force yourself to break the cycle. Pray that God will give you a new challenge, and then be alert to what that challenge might be. It might be as simple as a new hobby, a new exercise routine, or a renewed commitment to a daily devotional time. Or it might be something bigger, like starting a new business, agreeing to coach a church basketball team, or joining a new small group. To overcome depression, you usually don't need exemption from responsibility as much as you need a new opportunity. Don't seek security—seek to be stimulated by a new challenge.

When the children of Israel entered Canaan, they divided the land among the families, and everyone was clamoring for the prime real estate. Caleb came to Joshua to ask for the land that was due him. Remember Caleb? Forty years earlier, he was the only spy besides Joshua to bring back a good report when they first explored the land of Canaan. That's why Caleb and Joshua were the only ones of their generation allowed to enter the Promised Land. Now Caleb was eighty-five years old. Next to Joshua, he was the oldest person still alive among the Hebrews. He had earned the right to choose the best land—a paradise for his retirement years. Here's what he said to Joshua:

> Just as the LORD promised, he has kept me alive for forty-five years since the time he said this to Moses, while Israel moved about in the desert. So here I am today, eighty-five years old! I am still as strong today as the day Moses sent me out; I'm just as vigorous to go out to battle now as I was then. Now give me this hill country that the LORD promised me that day. You yourself heard then that the Anakites were there and their cities were large and fortified, but, the LORD helping me, I will drive them out just as he said. (Joshua 14:10–12)

What?! This eighty-five-year-old man could have said, "Give me that cushy valley over there where the enemy has already been driven out." Instead, he said, "I want that hill, and I don't care if there are wicked people living there—with God's help, I'll take it!" I hope I have that much spunk when I'm eighty-five years old! Caleb kept stretching and accepting new responsibility until the day he died. That may be one of the reasons he lived as long as he did.

Contrast Caleb with Florence Nightingale, the famous English nurse, who took to her bed at the age of fifty-six. She was convinced she would soon die of heart disease. She considered herself terminally ill and was a patient from that time on. She died when she was ninety. Had she gotten out of bed and taken on a new challenge, she wouldn't have   limited her effectiveness for thirty-four years of her life.

Jesus promised, "Be faithful, even to the point of death, and I will give you the crown of life" (Revelation 2:10).

Relationships

When God asked Elijah what he was doing way out in the desert, Elijah tried to explain his depression to God: "I have been very zealous for the LORD God Almighty. The Israelites have rejected your covenant, broken down your altars, and put your prophets to death with the sword. I am the only one left, and now they are trying to kill me too" (1 Kings 19:14). It's easy to see how Elijah could get depressed—he was exhausted, afraid, and alone.

After God gave Elijah some recuperation, a revelation, and a new responsibility, he also gave him a new relationship. He told Elijah to anoint a successor (Elisha) who would prove to be a great friend and supporter. Not only did the two men have similar names, but both also were men of faith. They had a oneness of spirit. Elijah began mentoring Elisha, and they developed a meaningful and lasting friendship.

God also told Elijah he was wrong about being alone. God knew of seven thousand Israelites who had not

bowed to Baal and who were willing to stand with
Elijah. God told him, "I reserve seven thousand in
Israel—all whose knees have not bowed down to Baal
and all whose mouths have not kissed him" (1 Kings
19:18). Elijah wasn't alone—he had *seven thousand*
allies!

Loneliness can be depressing. And the longer you're
depressed, the more tempted you are to keep friends at a
distance—which makes you more lonely, which makes
you more depressed. If you're battling depression, be alert
to the relationships God may provide for you, and don't
keep your friends at arm's length.

Make Some New Friends

If you've been depressed for an extended period of
time, it may be difficult for you to reconnect with old
friends. They may be leery of your sour moods. They may
worry that you'll return to your despair and shut them
out again. Maybe, like Elijah, you need to develop some
new friendships. You need to be faithful to family relationships, but outside of that, perhaps you can find some
friends who don't know your history—who will take your
comments at face value and who may be quicker to trust
you, inspire you, encourage you, and let you be yourself.
The Bible says, "Two are better than one, because they
have a good return for their work: If one falls down, his

friend can help him up. But pity the man who falls and has no one to help him up!" (Ecclesiastes 4:9–10).

Focus on Serving Others

Paul's letter to the Philippians contains tremendous advice on how to be joyful in the midst of difficult times. He wrote in Philippians 2:3–4, "Do nothing out of selfish ambition or vain conceit, but in humility consider others better than yourselves. Each of you should look not only to your own interests, but also to the interests of others."

Do you really want to get well? Do you really want to get over your depression? Are you willing to do what it takes to allow Jesus Christ and his Holy Spirit to transform your life? I have a prescription to help you. I'm so sure of its success that if I were a salesman, I'd put a high price on this prescription and offer a money-back guarantee. But I'm going to give it to you for free. (Well, except for the price of this book—maybe I'm not such a bad salesman after all!) Are you ready? Here it is: Do something to serve another person.

That's it! It's that simple. Quit thinking about you and your misery, and go serve someone who is in need. Don't wallow in self-pity anymore. Stop saying "No one wants to be around me" or "I can't do anything right." Self-pity is not humility—it's sin. It's a close relative of pride; both are self-centered thinking. "I can't... I don't have… Nobody wants me.…" All those phrases focus on one person—you. Determine to get your mind off yourself by doing something for somebody else. Mow someone's grass, take someone flowers, read for a school for the blind, donate money to a local charity, take your grandchildren to the park, wash your wife's car, visit a lonely person in a nursing home. Or get really radical and go on a short-term mission trip! Your life will never be the same!

If you can walk or talk or write or move your arms, you are capable of helping another person—and you're capable of overcoming your depression.

Jesus said, "Whoever wants to save his life will lose it, but whoever loses his life for me will find it" (Matthew 16:25) and "The greatest among you will be your servant. For whoever exalts himself will be humbled, and whoever humbles himself will be exalted" (Matthew 23:11–12).

Dr. Robert Tuttle, a professor of evangelism at Asbury Theological Seminary, related a story about a nine-year-old boy named Paul who accidentally wet his pants while sitting at his desk at school. Suddenly there was a puddle between his feet, and the front of his pants was soaked. He was devastated. It had never happened to him before, but he knew that when the kids found out, he would be the laughingstock of the class. His heart pounded as he prayed, "Dear God, this is an emergency! I need help right now!"

When Paul looked up, the teacher was walking toward him. He was about to be discovered. But walking just ahead of the teacher was one of Paul's classmates, Suzie, carrying a goldfish bowl filled with water. Suzie tripped in front of the teacher and dumped the water in Paul's lap!

Paul pretended to be angry, all the while whispering in his heart, "Thank you, Jesus! Thank you, Jesus!" Instead of being the object of ridicule, Paul was the object of sympathy. The teacher rushed downstairs to get him a pair of gym shorts to wear while his pants were drying out. When he returned, the ridicule that should have been his was being transferred to someone else—Suzie. She tried to help mop up the mess, but the kids kept saying, "You've done enough, you klutz!" As the day went on, the sympathy for Paul grew, and the ridicule of Suzie got worse.

It was the end of the day, while the students were waiting at the bus stop, that Paul figured it out. The other children were still shunning Suzie, but Paul approached her and whispered, "Suzie, you did that on purpose, didn't you?"

She whispered back, "I wet my pants once too."

If you're depressed, look for someone in dire circumstances and take some dramatic steps to help him or her. When you reach out and serve someone else, you'll be amazed at how much comfort you receive in return. The Bible says that God "comforts us in all our troubles, so that we can comfort those in any trouble with the comfort we ourselves have received from God" (2 Corinthians 1:4).

The night before he was crucified, Jesus took time to

explain to his disciples what was about to happen. In the midst of his final words to his disciples before his death, he said, "I have told you this so that my joy may be in you and that your joy may be complete" (John 15:11). Though Jesus knew that each of the disciples, and he most of all, was about to endure incredible suffering, he was able to talk about joy. How could he do it? Because Jesus knew that joy has nothing to do with your circumstances and everything to do with your attitude. And you never lose the power to choose your own attitude.

When you know the end of the story—that the victory will be won and that the days of pain will result in an eternity of happiness—you can "rejoice in the Lord always" (Philippians 4:4). Does that mean you'll always be happy? Does it mean you'll never face difficulty, never mourn the loss of someone you love, never get angry, never battle depression? No way. But it does mean that even in the midst of your sorrow, you can trust that your Savior will give you hope, and peace, and even joy.

PRAYER **Starter:**

Dear Father, sometimes this world can be a cruel place, and I long for the day when you'll come and make all things right. I know you don't expect me to be happy all the time. Thank you for loving me no matter what mood I'm in. But Lord, you've called me to be a person of joy. Help me today to "rejoice always" in you, regardless of my circumstances. When I'm down, Lord, reveal yourself to me and remind me that you are "an ever-present help in trouble" (Psalm 46:1). May people see in me a spirit of joy regardless of the circumstances around me. Please give me an attitude adjustment today, Lord, that the joy of Christ may be in me and reflected to those around me.

DISCUSSION Questions

1. How prone are you to periods of despondency? What causes you to get depressed? In which category are those causes? Is it your temperament? Circumstances? Physical or psychological causes?

2. When you're down, how do you react? How does it affect your family and close friends? When you're depressed, what can your family and close friends do to help you? What should they not do or say?

3. What was the worst period of depression you've ever experienced? How long did it last? What caused it? How did you rise out of it? What did you learn from it?

4. How do you overcome depression? Which of the steps in the last section of the chapter are usually the most helpful for you?

5. On a scale of one to ten, how joyful are you right now? What needs to change in your life to make you higher on the "joy scale"? Do your circumstances really need to change, or do you just need to adjust your attitude?

NOTES

Introduction

1. This story is true, but fictitious names have been added for readability and to protect the privacy of those involved.

2. Max Lucado, *Grace for the Moment: Inspirational Thoughts for Each Day of the Year* (Nashville: Thomas Nelson, Inc., 2000), 36.

Chapter 1: From Griping to Grateful

1. Johnson Oatman, Jr., and Edwin Othello Excell, "Count Your Blessings" (1897).

Chapter 2: From Worry to Peace

1. Apparently The Worry Company is defunct, since we couldn't locate it when we searched for documentation. Perhaps they have enough worries of their own!

2. Jim Miller, Elsie Osborn and Jack Osborn, "Where the Roses Never Fade" © 1942 Stamps-Baxter Music (BMI; admin. by Brentwood-Benson Music Publishing, Inc.) All rights reserved. Used by permission.

3. Quoted in Charles R. Swindoll, *The Finishing Touch* (Dallas: Word Publishing, 1994), 124–25.

Chapter 3: From Bitterness to Forgiveness

1. Lewis Smedes, *Forgive and Forget* (Carmel, Calif.: Guideposts, with special arrangement with Harper & Row, 1984), 2.

2. Ibid., 124.

3. Colin Brown, "Sin," *New International Dictionary of New Testament Theology, vol. 3* (Grand Rapids: Zondervan, 1986), 577. By the time the New Testament was written, *hamartia* may or may not have held the same meaning— we don't know for sure. But the illustration still applies. In our sin we miss the mark of God's perfection.

4. Elvina M. Hall and John T. Grape, "Jesus Paid It All" (1917).

5. Horatio Gates Spafford and Philip Paul Bliss, "It Is Well with My Soul" (1873).

6. John R. W. Stott, *The Message of the Sermon on the Mount* (Downers Grove, Ill.: InterVarsity Press, 1978), 149.

7. Max Lucado, *The Great House of God* (Dallas: Word Publishing, 1997), 120–21.

8. Lewis Smedes, *Forgive and Forget*, 2. Please note: We changed some of the terms in Smedes' four stages of forgiveness, but the concept of the four stages and the explanations are Mr. Smedes'.

9. David Jeremiah, *Prayer: The Great Adventure* (Sisters, Ore.: Multnomah Publishers, 1997), 149.

10. Les Parrott and Leslie Parrott, *When Bad Things Happen to Good Marriages* (Grand Rapids: Zondervan, 2001), 141.

11. James Dobson, *Love Must Be Tough* (Dallas: Word Publishing, 1983).

12. Jan Frank, *Door of Hope: Recognizing and Resolving the Pains of Your Past* (Nashville: Thomas Nelson, Inc., 1995).

13. Henry Cloud and John Townsend, *Boundaries: When to Say Yes, When to Say No, to Take Control of Your Life* (Grand Rapids: Zondervan, 1992).

14. John D. Beckett, *Loving Monday* (Downers Grove, Ill.: InterVarsity Press, 1998), 102–103.

Chapter 4: From Depression to Joy

1. "Prozac at 5," *U.S. News & World Report*, 9 December, 1996.

2. Les Carter, *Mind Over Emotions* (Grand Rapids: Baker Book House, 1985), 38–39.

3. Ibid., 39.

4. National Center for Health Statistics, "Suicide Among Older Persons—United States 1980–1992" <http://www.cdc.gov/mmwr/preview/mmwrhtml/0003993 7.htm>

5. Philip Zimbardo, "The Age of Indifference," *Psychology Today*, August 1980, 70–76.

6. David Burns, quoted by Edward Ziegler, "Think Your Way Out of Depression," *Readers' Digest*, December 1980, 124–27.

7. Frank Minirth, M.D., and Paul Meier, M.D., *Happiness Is a Choice* (Grand Rapids: Baker Book House, 1978), 21.

8. Jack Canfield et al., *Chicken Soup for the Soul at Work* (Deerfield Beach, Fla.: Health Communications, Inc., 1996), 211–13.